Selling with Soul

*Achieving Career Success
without Sacrificing
Personal and Spiritual Growth*

Sharon V. Parker

iUniverse, Inc.
Bloomington

Selling with Soul, Version 2.0
Achieving Career Success without Sacrificing
Personal and Spiritual Growth

First Publication Copyright © 2004 by Sharon V. Parker
Version 2.0 Copyright © 2012 by Sharon V. Parker

All rights reserved. No part of this book may be used or reproduced by any means, graphic, electronic, or mechanical, including photocopying, recording, taping or by any information storage retrieval system without the written permission of the publisher except in the case of brief quotations embodied in critical articles and reviews.

The views expressed in this work are solely those of the author and do not necessarily reflect the views of the publisher, and the publisher hereby disclaims any responsibility for them.

iUniverse books may be ordered through booksellers or by contacting:

iUniverse
1663 Liberty Drive
Bloomington, IN 47403
www.iuniverse.com
1-800-Authors (1-800-288-4677)

Because of the dynamic nature of the Internet, any web addresses or links contained in this book may have changed since publication and may no longer be valid. The views expressed in this work are solely those of the author and do not necessarily reflect the views of the publisher, and the publisher hereby disclaims any responsibility for them.

Any people depicted in stock imagery provided by Thinkstock are models, and such images are being used for illustrative purposes only.

Certain stock imagery © Thinkstock.

ISBN: 978-1-4697-5328-7 (sc)
ISBN: 978-1-4697-5327-0 (hc)
ISBN: 978-1-4697-5329-4 (e)

Library of Congress Control Number: 2012901659

Printed in the United States of America

iUniverse rev. date: 2/14/2012

To my husband and soul mate, Joel Parker, whose encouragement and unconditional love made this book possible. I also want to thank my father for giving me a voracious love of books and my mother for giving me the tenacity to achieve my goals and a work ethic that has brought me success in my work and my life. I also want to dedicate this work to Megan, my daughter, who is the creative work of which I am most proud; my son-in-law Stefan; my best friend, Camille; and all the members of my family for all the love and lessons we have shared. Since the first edition of this book, Finneas William Larkin has entered my life. To my ultimate grandson, I say you have all the powers to infinity plus nine. Love rules.

Every soul has to learn the whole lesson for itself. It must go over the whole ground. What it does not see, what it does not live, it will not know.
—Ralph Waldo Emerson,
Journal, October 2, 1837

Contents

FOREWORD xi

PREFACE
What's a Nice Person Like Me Doing in a Job Like This? xv

ACKNOWLEDGMENTS xxi

INTRODUCTION
To The Revised And Expanded Second Edition xxiii

CHAPTER 1
What Is Sales? 1

CHAPTER 2
A Day In The Life 7

CHAPTER 3
First, Do No Harm: The Company And Product You Represent . 13

CHAPTER 4
The Matter Of Personal Styles 25

CHAPTER 5
How People Buy Today 31

CHAPTER 6
Sales Basics 41

CHAPTER 7
Getting The First Appointment 47

CHAPTER 8
Qualifying: Respecting Yourself And Your Customer 61

CHAPTER 9
Presenting Your Solution 73

CHAPTER 10
Discovering And Responding To Concerns 79

CHAPTER 11
The Importance Of Listening 89

CHAPTER 12
The "Close" And Why It's Really The Opening 99

CHAPTER 13
Managing Growth Through Conflict 109

CHAPTER 14
Temptations And Compromising Situations. 117

CHAPTER 15
The Importance Of Spiritual Role Models. 125

AFTERWORD
A Few Final Thoughts 133

A Gift for my Readers 135

BIBLIOGRAPHY 137

FOREWORD

By
Don H. Davis, Jr.
Chairman and Chief Executive Officer
Rockwell

ALL OF US IN business today know that the old models are changing. New technology is driving much of that change, speeding up the process of buying and selling and challenging all of us to develop more effective ways of working. But a subtler change is taking place, too, in the way people feel about working.

For some, adapting to change is stressful. For others, it means an opportunity for creativity. Some of us feel energized by the challenge, while others feel drained and overwhelmed by demands on their time and energy that seem constantly increasing. More and more people are changing careers, either because of economic or technological changes in their former line of work or because they're seeking more job satisfaction.

If change is unavoidable, and sometimes desirable, the only question is whether, and how, you manage the changes in your life to produce the results you want.

What makes a job or a career fulfilling? The same thing that makes any activity satisfying: it must allow you to express who you are, your true character, your values, and your interests. If you're doing something that violates who you are or what you believe in, then you're going to be unhappy. But if your job allows you to use your strengths, be yourself, and respect yourself at the end of the day, then your work will be fulfilling. Sharon Parker calls that "work with soul."

The French writer and dramatist Albert Camus once said, "Without work, all life goes rotten; but when work is soulless, life stifles and dies." We all need to work, and we need work that expresses who we are. We need the opportunity to be creative, to feel useful, to make a contribution to someone or something beyond ourselves, and to be appreciated for what we add to the team effort. We need the opportunity to express ourselves honestly and to know we're heard and respected.

These experiences add what you might call "human value" to our work lives. A work environment that provides multiple human needs—social, emotional, and spiritual, as well as financial—gives us the opportunity to do our best work, to succeed personally as well as professionally. That's the kind of environment that attracts and retains valuable employees. It's the kind of workplace every executive wants to build and maintain.

But creating the ideal work environment isn't the responsibility of executives and managers alone. They can set the tone and uphold values like integrity and cooperation and mutual support. But the power—and the responsibility—to create the world in which we work and live lies with each of us.

We begin by choosing our field or profession, and then our employer and job. Every day, we create an environment of trust or suspicion, conflict or cooperation, depending on how we treat others. I tell those who want to know how to be an effective leader to start by developing their own character. Surround yourself with people you can trust and admire, and become one yourself. Build business relationships on integrity, concern for others, and willingness to take risk and shoulder responsibility. These qualities of character will attract and inspire others who share those values. Together you can become an unbeatable professional team.

I've worked in every level of business from sales trainee to CEO, and I can tell you that creating long-term success requires more than turning a profit. Successful businesses are built on trust, cooperation, and support, not conflict, deceit, and manipulation. Profits are necessary and contribute not only to the well-being of shareholders and employees, but through them to society as a whole. You can't create long-term profits without creating a place where people want to work and a workforce that regards its members as human beings, not roles on an organizational chart. People who find satisfaction at work will do their jobs well and help the company succeed.

All business is built on sales. None of us would be in business without the people who buy our products and services. Yet the salesperson often ranks last in respect within the business world, as well as in society as a whole.

Robert Louis Stevenson once wrote, "Everyone lives by selling something." We all sell our talents and skills, our services, time, labor, and personality. Yet we've built a negative connotation around the profession of selling, not because we object to trading goods and services for money but because we associate selling with trading our principles for material gain. We say a person "sells out" when he violates his own principles for material gain, or "sells his soul" when he trades his integrity for money.

But this isn't what sales has to be. Like any activity, selling can be as worthwhile and valuable as you make it. If you invest it with your character, those values you want to express at work as you do at home, you are adding "human value" to the sales process. And that's what customers really buy—not just a product or service, but the human value you offer along with it. That's *Selling with Soul*.

This is not trading our principles, but trading *with* principle. When an auto dealer sells integrity and a plumber sells good service, they don't relinquish what they've sold, because integrity and service are internal human values. Their customers only pay for short-term use. They could buy the same car from a different dealer or call a different plumber to fix the sink. But what they're buying is not just a car or plumbing—it's the human value that the seller adds to it.

When you sell *with* soul, as opposed to selling your soul, your reputation is enhanced. Your value to your customer is increased. You succeed, and the company you represent succeeds with you.

Sharon Parker understood from the beginning of her sales career that the old guidelines—the ones that measured success only in dollars and cents—wouldn't work for her. She learned how to add "human value" to her work life, how to make it consistent with the person she is and make her career more satisfying.

Selling with Soul is an excellent guidebook for anyone in business, no matter what your position or career path, who wants to do the same.

PREFACE

What's a Nice Person Like Me Doing in a Job Like This?

To be successful, the first thing to do is fall in love with your work.
—Sister Mary Lauretta

WHEN A CAREER COUNSELOR first recommended I consider a job in sales, I looked down at my tailored suit and mentally reviewed my makeup and jewelry, trying to pinpoint what made him think I was sleazy. I ranked salespeople just behind ambulance chasers on my ethical scale. Why would anyone want such a job? The obvious answer, according to that same counselor, was "For the money!" As a single parent climbing out of debt from a failed marriage, that was an attractive incentive, but selling was not for me.

The job counselor painted a glossy picture of success: custom suits and Italian shoes, a company-provided Cadillac, and dining at four-star restaurants. But I was haunted by stereotypes. I remember thinking that many an alleged organized crime leader wears thousand-dollar suits and gets photographed at black-tie society events. That didn't mean I want to be one.

Salespeople, in my mind, were pushy, greedy, self-serving, and more than willing to tell a half-truth or an outright lie to get the sale. I thought of the job itself as pressuring, manipulating, and convincing people to buy things they don't need, often with money they don't have. If the world's oldest profession is prostitution, then the world's first "professionals" were selling, and I was embarrassed remembering how often I'd heard the slang terms for prostitutes applied to salespeople.

On the other hand, I had bills to pay and a child to raise, and I needed a job. I thought sales could be a good temporary solution. So in my crisp navy suit and well-polished low heels, my silk scarf bowed, and my savings account nearly empty, I set off. Every one of my first three sales interviews resulted in a job offer. Dizzy with my newfound success, I weighed my choices and selected a company with a good reputation, formal training program, and base salary in addition to commission. It was the eighties, and there were still secretaries and stenographers tending to the day-to-day running of business communications using typewriters. Personal computers, Internet communications, and online research were still dreams in the minds of people like Steve Jobs and Bill Gates. For the era, the company I chose was on the leading edge. I would be selling word processors and minicomputers to technology-challenged businesspeople. I bought some new suits and quashed the fear, based on my own stereotypes about sales, that I was starting down a path that would start with selling product but end with selling my soul.

My first day came, and I met my peers. This in no way reassured me. If you are a fan of *Mad Men* on the AMC channel, you have seen a good example of the business world I entered. The top salesman was a chain-smoking "veteran," who made it clear I'd better not come near his accounts. The other salesman was a young man so full of himself he nearly burst out of his Oxford shirt. He offered to teach me everything I needed to know. Since he'd been on the job three months, I figured it wouldn't take long. My sales manager, a good-looking man with a flirtatious manner and a tendency to touch me often, was no help. I give thanks regularly that this atmosphere is no longer acceptable in business. Back then, I accepted that it was normal.

I was eager to start the training program, since I knew nothing about selling but took pride in being a quick learner. After the four weeks, I still knew nothing about selling, but had learned every picayune feature and detail of my product line. I was pumped. I left convinced my word processors belonged on every desk in the corporate world. My product would make secretaries and administrative staff more efficient, executives more productive and cheerful, eliminate disease, and end world hunger. I soon received the rest of my training at the hands of my prospective customers. They pointed out features my product lacked and where it fell short of the competition. My inflated confidence sprang a leak, and instead of "hitting the ground running," my ego deflated and I hit the ground hard.

When I picked myself back up, remembering I still had bills to pay, I asked more questions of my customers and listened carefully to their answers. From them I developed a thorough understanding of my product, what problems it solved, and where it failed to provide a solution. Listening to my customers taught me more than any product training could.

The second half of my training program was devoted to sales technique. I sat through a twenty-four-videotape version of Tom Hopkins's *How to Master the Art of Selling* and was handed a copy of Zig Ziglar's *See You at the Top*. I dutifully memorized power closes word-for-word and developed a "script" for telephone prospecting. I taped a mirror to my telephone to remind myself to smile and trained myself to say a warm thank you to the dead phone after someone hung up on me.

Out in the real world, I soon abandoned the baggage of scripts and closes. I realized I was already a better listener than most of my colleagues and that when I used that skill, the customer told me what the problem was and helped me decide how best to solve it. Whether through nature or nurture, I was good at putting myself in the customer's shoes. I began to build relationships with customers. I got to know the support and field service people who were my life preservers in a sea roiled by inconsistent product quality. And I learned to keep a roll of Tums in my purse and a bottle of Maalox at my desk.

My income doubled. Then tripled. Sooner than I would have dreamed possible, I came to consider six figures to be a realistic and attainable goal. But I was not happy. As the technology advanced, I changed companies, becoming more knowledgeable about software, networks, and communications technology. It was now the late nineties, and while I had updated my fashions, my music, and my tastes, selling was still selling. I won awards. I became a well-known and respected consultative salesperson in my field. But I was not happy. Although I enjoyed working with my customers, I hated introducing myself as a "salesperson." I felt I was carrying the weight of all the sales stereotypes and all the negative images of corporate America on my shoulders. I wanted to do work that mattered, that made a difference. And it seemed impossible to do that within the Fortune 1000.

My soul was hungry. I tried to feed it by volunteering on a crisis line. I spoke at self-help groups and mentored. It wasn't enough. I longed to teach or do social work, even considering training as a lay minister/family counselor so I could do work every day that I perceived as having intrinsic value and that I considered congruent with my spiritual needs. When I realized I did not have the credentials for those jobs, I aggressively pursued "business" positions in social service agencies as marketing director, development director or fund-raiser, and executive director. But there were many people qualified to do those jobs who had worked their way up in social service and had stronger credentials than mine. It was déjà vu—a familiar pattern of interviews followed by rejection letters.

Then I experienced what Jung called synchronicity and my family would call luck. Returning from a business meeting, I sat next to a fellow employee from another office, someone whose success I admired. I asked him what made him successful, expecting to hear about techniques and "tricks" of the trade. Instead, he talked about integrity and the daily challenge of maintaining it within corporations driven by stockholders' demands for short-term results. He expressed frustration at the split between his business and personal lives and shared with me his longing to integrate his spiritual growth into his daily work.

My mind was racing as we said our good-byes; and when I got to my car, I pulled out my notebook and hurried to capture my thoughts. I asked myself: Is it possible to integrate selling with spiritual principles? Could I be a force for change within the corporate world? Could I integrate work and home, job and spirit, and help others to do the same? I had more questions than answers, but at least I knew now that I was not alone in wanting to find a way to heal the split between work and family, values and common business practices, career growth and spiritual growth. Through trial and error over the next ten years, I learned the answer to the questions is yes. I have found and worked with many people who share this goal, and I have learned that salespeople have unique opportunities to grow spiritually within their jobs. We are also well positioned to lead change in our companies.

The movement to bring "soul" to work began in the nineties with business writers like Stephen Covey, Ken Blanchard, and Tom Peters, who recognized the need to transform business by bringing spiritual values and business practices in line. Americans grab up books like *Chicken Soup for the Soul at Work* hoping for an answer. But while many are focused on business in general, the fundamental business of business remains buying and selling, and sales remains a well-defended bastion of "all's fair in love and war" thinking.

I've thrown out my old sales training books. I laugh at the scripts and closes I memorized. I approach every customer as an individual and every opportunity as a chance to serve. Every meeting offers lessons in listening, learning, compassion, and respect. I, like most professional salespeople, am a problem solver. Together with my customer, I create value. I create value for my customers even when I tell them my product is not the best solution and recommend they seek another approach. I face conflict head-on and with empathy, and I do my work with integrity. When I feel a twinge of conscience or discomfort, I no longer reach for the antacid but instead find a quiet place to close my eyes and listen to my inner wisdom, the voice of spirit. I have lost sales, but I have rarely lost a customer.

I understand that many people are better qualified than I to teach, counsel, or minister. But until recently, few were qualified and willing to stay within the corporate world as what the late thought leader and author Peter Drucker called "change leaders."

Today I work with sales representatives who provide a wide range of hardware, software, and services, primarily to manufacturers. Their products impact the very point of production and can make or break a customer's profitability for a day, a shift, or longer. It is a challenge and a joy to work with people who are committed to doing their best for their customers, to helping solve the problem or get out of the way. With this book, *Selling with Soul*, I challenge salespeople, both rookies and veterans, to rediscover pride in our work as we declare today and every day "bring your soul to work" day.

ACKNOWLEDGMENTS

I WISH TO ACKNOWLEDGE the contribution of Don H. Davis, Jr., chairman and CEO of Rockwell, for contributing the foreword to the first edition. I am including it in this revised version because Don's thought leadership continues to be valuable and successful. Don has always led with courage and with soul.

I also wish to acknowledge Jerry Greenfield, cofounder of Ben & Jerry's Homemade, who provided a review for the book jacket. Jerry continues to be a leader for social responsibility in the business world today.

I also wish to acknowledge Michael T. Bosworth, thought leader and author, for his many contributions to advancing the sales profession and generously sharing his wisdom.

INTRODUCTION

To The Revised And Expanded Second Edition

ALL OF US "SELL," regardless of job title—from the minister in the pulpit to the classroom teacher to your neighbor collecting money for charity. We sell in our daily lives when we negotiate vacation plans with our spouse or a new division of household chores with our teenager. And in corporations, everybody sells regardless of position. Human resource managers sell proposed policies and head-count plans. Financial managers sell their proposed budgets. Engineers sell their proposed designs and justify spending company funds on development costs. And all of us sell ourselves. Anyone who reports to a manager knows that the ability to promote your contributions and value to your boss is pivotal at salary review time. The ability to sell yourself and your ideas may be the most essential skill for achieving business success. And yet, our society demeans selling and salespeople, perpetuating stereotypes that make us cringe.

The goals of this book are to attack those attitudes head-on, to help you learn the skills and attitudes that result in successful sales careers, and to share the life lessons that can result in a successful, balanced life as well—lessons I learned the hard way over twenty-six years in sales.

The first step to improving a process is to understand the process. For that reason, the book includes a review of sales basics, updated with how people buy today. The Internet has had a major impact on our profession and on the buying cycle, and we need to adapt and embrace this change to be successful. The book also shares ideas for finding and keeping new business, and lessons in the soft skills so essential to selling with integrity and empathy: listening, conflict resolution, understanding personal styles, dealing with temptations and compromise, and creating a life consistent with your values.

Since the first edition of this book in 2001, our world has changed in ways we could not have foreseen: the terrorist attacks on 9/11, the wars in Iraq and Afghanistan, the collapse of mortgage banking, corporate bailouts, and high levels of unemployment. Stress and the toll it takes on our physical and mental health is well-documented. But what about the stress on our souls?

In the face of these crises, it is often as difficult to keep our values front and center as it is for a captain to keep his bearings in a stormy sea. But, as self-help author Shakti Gawain puts it, "Every time you don't follow your inner guidance, you feel a loss of energy, loss of power, a sense of spiritual deadness."

This book has been expanded and updated to reflect changes in culture, technology, and social mores, but its original purpose remains: It is intended to help heal the splits between the demands of our jobs and the needs of our families, our work and our passions, our values and our rationalized actions. For every salesperson out there who feels embarrassed by what she does for a living or who adopts an attitude of cynicism as a protective shield for her aching soul, this book was written for you. It will help you see the value of what you do for a living and a way to do it with pride. Here's to a satisfying career selling with soul.

CHAPTER 1

What Is Sales?

SELLING AT ITS SIMPLEST is solving problems. None of us buy products. We buy a solution to a problem we can't solve ourselves. If someone tried to sell me a green plastic tube, I'd laugh. But once it became clear that the tube could deliver water from the faucet to my rose garden, I would give him my full attention. The seller who understands the customer's problem, who honestly educates the customer as to why his or her product or service will solve it, and who stands behind that solution with after-sale involvement is a sales professional. In fact, if after careful consideration, such a seller believes his product or service will not solve the problem, he says so. He may even refer the customer to another supplier who can help.

Selling is described as a series of steps, from prospecting to closing, that lead to success measured in income. What gets left out of that description are the pressures put on salespeople every day. We are pressured to push the product of the month even if it may not be best for the job, to promote a product even though it still has major "bugs," to downplay or not mention problems with deliveries, to jack up the price so we can appear to give a deep discount, to create artificial "deadlines" or fire sales to goad a customer into making a decision. The atmosphere that surrounds sales takes a toll on the salesperson. Tension headaches, ulcers, sleepless nights, burnout, and conflicts at home are the too common results. Sales managers who greet each sales success with "But what have you done for me lately?" add to the needless pressure.

This book takes aim at the stereotypes and the toxic atmosphere that surround the sales professional. We will look at the basic steps from a broader perspective intended to help salespeople find joy in what they do and balance in their lives. Instead of just offering techniques, we will look at the attitudes that transform the steps and allow us to sell with soul. Selling benefits more than the seller and the buyer. Selling creates jobs. It is a primary business driver, adding value to our economy. When sales plummet, companies cut back. When sales exceed forecasts, companies expand. Selling is the lifeblood of business.

Product design can't create jobs. It won't take you long to think of several examples of brilliant products that failed commercially, even products that were technically superior to their competition. TiVO, for example, offered state-of-the-art technology that replaced the cable box and allowed television viewers to record four channels at once, rewind live TV, skip commercials, and more, yet the cable providers continue to expand their leases of functionally-limited boxes and DVRs. In 1972, DuPont researchers invented Kevlar, a material as lightweight and strong as iron, and considered it the most important new fiber since nylon. Expecting to reap the profits from a billion-dollar market, they watched in disappointment for more than a decade as the market failed to grow beyond the need for bulletproof vests and sports equipment. They needed salespeople to find problems Kevlar could solve. Today, Kevlar is in the body of the Motorola Droid, cookware, audio systems, brake linings, drumheads, and woodwind reeds, all as a result of creative sales and marketing.

Promotion and advertising won't create jobs. When Apple launched the MacIntosh, it bought the most expensive advertising available. Its innovative ad titled "1984" showed unthinking drones following Big Brother, or "Big Blue," but it failed to stop the rising tide of less-efficient IBM clones from dominating the market. The resulting job losses at Apple extended all the way up to the founder of the company, the late Steve Jobs, who resigned in 1985 from the company he created.

Dropping your price won't create jobs—it may even cause buyers to question a product's value based on the "you get what you pay for" axiom. And "place," how you get your product to market, is not the answer. Your successes will be quickly imitated, and you will soon find yourself sharing shelf space or distributors with your competitors.

Many brilliant people have failed to appreciate the value of selling. Even a former industry icon like the late Ken Olsen, founder of Digital

Equipment Corporation and former *Fortune* magazine "Man of the Century," was reputed to consider salespeople unnecessary. Folklore has it he maintained throughout his reign that a really good catalog would do more for company growth than the best sales staff.

Today's "visionaries" argue that a great website and electronic commerce will replace salespeople as the best way to match goods and services with buyers. And yet, an entire industry exists just to provide training seminars and skills improvement classes to salespeople. Marketing expert Philip Kotler, in his perennially popular textbook *Marketing Management*, sums it up best by pointing out that "Today's companies spend hundreds of millions of dollars each year to train their salespeople in the art of salesmanship. Over a million copies of books, cassettes, and videotapes on selling are purchased annually." Why? Because at the end of the day, "People buy from people."

As sales veterans know, the tangible benefits of a career in sales include above-average income, flexibility and autonomy, and potential for rapid advancement. Salespeople rank high on annual salary surveys. In 2011, Salary.com reported average earnings of $78,218 for account sales reps, $64,900 for starting sales reps, and $122,700 for top sales executives. Compare that with the starting salary for most engineers of $66,124, and sales looks very profitable—especially since no formal schooling beyond a four-year degree or equivalent industry experience is required. Sales managers, according to similar "what you're worth" surveys, can earn $100,000 to $165,000 depending on industry.

Salespeople often cite their relative autonomy, their ability to set their own hours, establish their own priorities, and remain flexible in the face of family demands, as benefits of their career. At a time when national surveys validate a growing desire among professionals to work fewer and more flexible hours, this fact, especially when combined with high earnings potential, would seem to make sales a highly desirable career. As a single parent, I valued being able to chaperone a field trip or attend a midday school program for my daughter. My schedule was mine to manage, and my sales manager was only concerned with my results.

But despite the benefits to the individual and to the economy, few college graduates aspire to be salespeople. Corporations lament that it is increasingly difficult to recruit and retain sales professionals. As reported on www.cnbc.com, "As companies shift their focus to growth mode, they need more people out on the front lines driving revenue growth and that means they need to boost their sales teams. A whopping 27 percent of hiring managers said they plan to hire for sales positions in 2011, according to the CareerBuilder survey."

Companies are in desperate need of salespeople who, as Stephen Covey, author of *The 7 Habits of Highly Effective People,* describes it, "solve problems for an elite group of clients, using a mix of financial management and communication acumen." As 76.4 million retiring baby boomers are replaced, WhatsNextinYourLife.com predicts US businesses will experience a ten-million-person shortfall in filling sales positions. Why are sales professionals in such short supply?

The main barrier may be no more complicated than lingering stereotypes about salespeople and sales jobs. Many people think salespeople need a "killer instinct," with the competitive drive of a thoroughbred and the temperament of a pit bull. Sales is a war game, right? Sales managers and trainers are guilty of borrowing lingo from the military or competitive sports. The resulting slogans are adversarial, allowing for only one winner and demanding a loser. Slogans like Vince Lombardi's "Winning isn't everything—it's the only thing" remain popular, while ancient wisdom like "Caveat emptor" implies all salespeople should be required to wear a human version of the "Beware of Dog" sign.

Such attitudes, if they ever were helpful, are obsolete today. Selling is not adversarial. It is not war or sport. It is not all about the money, manipulation, or creation of false need. In fact, the seller operating from this paradigm will fail over the long term. Whether you measure sales success by income, recognition, or job satisfaction, it can only be achieved by working with your customers for mutual benefit. That is selling. Selling with soul goes beyond that to add the following elements, each of which will be discussed in later chapters. The elements of selling with soul include:

- Enjoying a balanced life where work and personal behavior are congruent
- Recognizing the importance of empathy
- Respecting yourself and your customer
- Practicing persistence and patience
- Listening to yourself and others with sensitivity
- Avoiding rationalization
- Embracing change
- Being a lifelong learner
- Achieving philosophical alignment

From preparation to prospecting to the ongoing maintenance and preservation of relationships built on trust and respect, selling with soul differentiates us and allows us to feel joy in what we do.

REFLECTIONS ON CHAPTER 1
What Is Sales?

Our deeds determine us, as much as we determine our deeds.
—George Eliot

The questions that follow are intended to begin a process of self-examination leading to rethinking sales. In this book, we will review each step in sales basics; but more importantly, we will reexamine those steps from the viewpoint of selling with soul and the qualities it requires, beginning with self-awareness. Each chapter will conclude with an opportunity for thoughtful reflection. Take a few minutes to jot down your thoughts and answers to the questions.

1. Why did you first go into sales? Who or what influenced you at the time you made that decision?
2. How do you regard your work today? Are you proud to announce when meeting new people that you sell for a living? If not, what is it you feel when asked about your job? Are you afraid of being stereotyped?
3. What do you most admire in salespeople you have worked with?
4. What do you most dislike in salespeople you have worked with?
5. Which of these characteristics do you see in yourself?

Note to Self: I practice my profession with pride and a willingness to constantly improve.

CHAPTER 2

A Day In The Life

You wake up only when the alarm buzzes. You roll over and hit the snooze button. Again. And again. It's Monday and time to go to work. You pull the sheets up to your chin and flip through the pages of your day planner in your mind, trying to find an appointment worth getting up for. There is that presentation at one o'clock, you remind yourself. You drag yourself out of bed, pull on your "uniform" of a business suit or today's "business casual," and kiss your partner and kids good-bye. Tucking your cell phone in your pocket, you head for the nearest espresso stand and pound a double-shot. You tell yourself this morning, as you do most mornings, that there's got to be a better way to live. There is.

It is common in today's culture to feel like jugglers, trying desperately to keep the plates spinning rather than crashing to the ground in pieces around us. Each plate represents a compartment in our fragmented lives, separated by numbers on our "to-do lists." We carry with us a constant feeling of having left something important undone. Our sleep is disrupted by anxiety over tomorrow's tasks or by recurring dreams about having missed the big test or having forgotten to pick up the kids from school. Stress and its many side effects have become a national epidemic, with WebMD (www.webmd.com/balance) reporting that 43 percent of all adults suffer from stress-related health issues and that 75 to 90 percent of all doctors' office visits are a result of stress-related effects on our health, such as headaches, high blood pressure, heart problems, diabetes, skin conditions, asthma, arthritis, depression, and anxiety. And it's not just a health issue but a financial one as well. The Occupational Safety and Health Administration (OSHA) estimates that stress costs American industry more than $300 billion annually.

We live in a culture that emphasizes the tangible and the material as the only means of keeping score. We have come to accept that work is the opposite of satisfying, the antithesis of our "real life." We know the words of the Chinese sage who recommended you find work you love and you'll never work a day in your life, but we shake our heads and wonder if he would have felt the same in the United States in 2011. We promise ourselves we'll do what we love when the kids are through school or when we retire. Even one of today's most successful capitalists and financiers, however, reminds us of an immutable truth. Warren Buffett, chairman of Berkshire Hathaway Inc., advised graduates to work for an organization they admired and not to be one of the people who do jobs they don't like, telling themselves that it's just temporary. He said, "I always worry about people who say, 'I'm going to do this for ten years; I really don't like it very well. And *then* I'll do this …' That's a little like saving up sex for your old age. Not a very good idea."

We hunger for a culture change and a life in which our whole selves have value, but changing a culture is difficult at best. Books on organizational behavior affirm that values are the most difficult to change, while behavior and habits may offer some opportunities for incremental growth. We must identify values and then provide ways to incorporate them into behavior.

When the Behavior Matches Values

One of my early sales role models was a man named Bob. Bob worked hard at his sales job. He had earned the highest ranking in our sales force, executive sales engineer, and consistently was top performer in the branch. Bob woke early each day, went to the gym, and exercised. Now, that might have been enough right there for me to resent him. After all, I've spent a lifetime trying to acquire that discipline and still only manage it sporadically. But it gets worse, or better, depending on your perspective.

Every morning before he began work, Bob took a few minutes to reflect, pray, or meditate. He aligned himself and his energies with his Higher Power and asked for guidance. Then, between the hours of 7:00 a.m. and 5:00 p.m., he was either doing follow-up letters and reports, working with a customer to solve a problem, or making phone calls and visits to potential new customers. Unlike many of us who met at lunch and complained about the customers of the morning, Bob used his lunchtime to get to know a customer better, never talking business during that time but instead learning more about the customers' families and interests outside of work. He had a rich family life and many interests of his own, and he delighted in sharing those and finding common ground with his customers.

By 6:00 p.m., Bob was home, where he and his wife took turns cooking. The kids worked on their homework or helped with meal preparation and household chores. At 7:00 p.m., they all sat down together for a meal. No one wore headphones to the table. No one grabbed food and ran out the door with it. This was a time when Bob and his wife would ask the kids about their day and share some highlights from their own. If the kids didn't want to talk, that was okay, but they knew they could count on the opportunity to do so and that their parents were willing to listen. Bob and his wife rarely told their children what to do, and I don't recall them ever stepping in and taking on one of their children's conflicts as their own. What they did instead was to be generous with their time, ask probing questions, and help their kids figure out what their choices were, as well as the likely consequences of each choice. They talked about their own values and beliefs, but never demanded their kids set the same priorities, believing that each child had to develop his or her own core of values and own spiritual foundation because no one can do that for another.

On those rare nights when Bob had to attend a seminar or customer event, he made sure to "catch up" with the family over breakfast the next morning. His day planner had the big events in their lives noted right next to his own appointments, so he never forgot to ask about the soccer game or the results of the drama club tryouts.

Bob's family attended church together on Sunday, but also routinely attended public lectures and forums on topics diverse and controversial on Sunday afternoons. His kids were encouraged to join in the debates that followed. Bob encouraged them to challenge ideas, ask thoughtful questions, and think creatively on any subject. Rather than being the "voice of authority," he shared his own opinions and ideas and his reasons for them while still listening respectfully to his kids when they disagreed. Bob and his wife were serious about "practicing" their beliefs as well and were involved in their church-sponsored meal program and in annual drives to raise funds for the needy.

Instead of giving each other expensive gifts at Christmas, Bob's family "adopted" someone more needy and enjoyed shopping together for clothing, household items, and toys for another family. Their own holiday time was full of traditions that meant a lot to all of them, many with jokes attached like trying to "stick" someone with the traveling fruitcake they had been passing among themselves for twelve years.

Dinner was a time of celebration and great thanks for all the love and blessings in their lives, with each member of the family offering a brief blessing before they all dug in.

He and his wife both bicycled and canoed, and the kids developed an interest in these activities as well, often choosing to spend a Saturday together exploring some new area on a day trip. The whole family shared an appreciation for the environment and the fragility of an ecosystem. There was a lot of friendly competition among them for who was the most fit in the sports they enjoyed.

When Bob retired early, there was no emptiness staring him in the face. His kids had all gone on to complete college and were busy in careers of their own. They gathered at holidays and spoke by telephone often. He and his wife were both more involved than ever in their private passions, hers for cross-cultural training within businesses and his for teaching technical classes at a community college. They continued to have community and church-related interests and to do volunteer work as a natural follow-up to their earlier activities.

I'd never met anyone as satisfied with his life as Bob, nor as balanced in his pursuit of a "full" life. His career and financial needs were met, and he took great pride in doing his job well. His family was a priority, and the love and respect they shared was apparent. His spiritual beliefs were evident in his integrity, his compassion, and his commitment of personal time to causes he believed in. He was physically fit and young for his years.

Bob made an excellent income, proving author Sharon Drew Morgen's assertion that working from personal spiritual values does not preclude making money. It does mean you'll make money congruently and consistently with your values, and support individual, group, company, and global change. For the past twenty years, Bob has been my image of a balanced and satisfying life. He sold with soul. He lived with soul. After many years, I now understand how he did it. How can you achieve Bob's balance?

I'll believe it when I see it, many of you may be thinking. I have seen it, in Bob and the others whom I've turned into a composite for this example. I've been fortunate to work with these people over the years. Is it magic? Only in the sense that Wayne Dyer describes it in his book, *I'll See It When I Believe It*.

Bob is a combination of several people I was privileged to work with over the past twenty years. I used to look at them with envy. Envy became admiration. Admiration led to a serious request that Bob "mentor" me and show me how he achieved such consistency between his personal and professional life. When the other sales reps said they wanted to be vice presidents some day or run their own business, I would smile and say, "I just want to be like Bob when I grow up!"

I learned a lot from him that continues to influence my priorities today, like the importance of taking care of myself. If you don't take care of yourself, how can you take care of others? That's why flight attendants tell you to put your own oxygen mask on first. He showed me the difference between urgent and important, and that what is truly important, family and friends, cannot be sacrificed repeatedly to the god of making money and survive. He taught me that people are people, not just customers, and the importance of respecting them and treating them with empathy. He taught me to be grateful every day for the blessing of my life. I'm sure Bob had days of doubt, an occasional loss of confidence, and dreams he let go of along the way, but he taught me the importance of going inside myself and listening respectfully and sympathetically to what my soul was telling me. He taught me to use my values as "true north" to reset my compass and stay on course. That's what selling—and living—with soul are all about.

REFLECTIONS ON CHAPTER 2
A Day in the Life

The only measure of what you believe is what you do. If you want to know what people believe, don't read what they write, don't ask them what they believe, just observe what they do.
—Ashley Montagu

To achieve Bob's balance, you have to first know what matters to you. It's not what other people have told you to do, not what other people expect from you, not the long list of "should" you may have grown up with, but what *you* truly care about. Here are some questions to help identify your values so that you can begin to live and work in harmony with them.

1. Describe your perfect weekend or vacation day, start to finish. Who would you spend it with? How much time would you want to spend alone? What activities would you choose?
2. Describe your perfect workday, and compare the two.
3. If you were told you had only five more years to live, how would you change your life? What would you want people to say about you in your eulogy?

Note to Self: I can choose to live in balance.

CHAPTER 3

First, Do No Harm: The Company And Product You Represent

ARE YOU PROUD OF your employer? Doctors take an oath to "first, do no harm." Selling with soul demands the same commitment. But how far does our control extend? How much responsibility do we have for our company's actions, our customer's actions, and the unforeseeable outcomes?

Our first challenge is to look at our company as an entity with a life and purpose that affects the larger community. How does your company define its mission? No doubt the company has spent a great deal of time and money writing an official mission statement and then publicizing it, both inside and outside the company. In fact, there's probably a great-looking framed version of it hanging on the lobby wall right this minute. Beyond its decorative impact, however, a mission statement is intended to help everyone in the company focus on one central purpose. It is a banner behind which we are expected to march in step, even if too often only lip service is paid to the words.

Selling with soul requires that we not only examine the mission statement of the company we choose to represent, but that we have one of our own. Here is mine:

I put integrity first in all my client dealings. I seek to understand my client's goals before offering ideas. Only after I have understanding and empathy for my client's position do I offer my own views. I am committed to lifelong learning so that I can be of the best service possible to everyone with whom I do business. I am responsible to my clients as well as to my family, friends, and society to do the best I can and to use my talents to make the world a better place, one step at a time.

My own mission statement reflects my values, and yours needs to be built on your own principles and beliefs. In the questions for reflection at the end of this chapter, you will have an opportunity to explore and further define your mission.

The emphasis in most mission statements is responsibility to the various stakeholders, including employees, customers, shareholders, and community. But what if your company does not walk its own talk? What if the day-to-day at your employer feels a lot like your parents saying, "Do as I say, not as I do"? It is this kind of contradiction that survey respondents must have had in mind when they questioned the ethics and the community involvement of business today.

If the mission statement of your company is worthy of respect, your task becomes one of reminding everyone you interact with that decisions should be held up to the mirror of your mission to see if they reflect well or poorly on you. If the company is serious about living up to its mission, it may provide ombudsmen or ad hoc committees and task forces whose job it is to monitor problems and help get actions back in line with the stated guidelines. Becoming part of this effort is one way to see for yourself if the company "puts its money where its mouth is."

An ongoing discussion in one of my LinkedIn groups asks the question, "Can you sell a product you don't believe in?" The cliché description of a peddler was that "he could sell refrigerators to Eskimos." The implication, of course, is that a good salesperson can sell things to people who don't need them. The salesperson with soul responds, "But why?" Why would you want to sell something the customer didn't need or wouldn't benefit from? I'm not talking here about luxury items or "toys" or other indulgences like that little red sports car you drool over or the cabin cruiser I've always dreamed about. Everyone blessed with earning more than he or she needs indulges in some discretionary spending, hopefully after remembering to save for future needs. Spending in this category is always based more on "want" than "need," a distinction most of us figure out sometime after three years old. There is nothing wrong with purchases for pleasure, but most salespeople are tasked with helping a customer solve a problem and doing so in a way that provides a good return on the money spent.

Returning to the selling of "refrigerators to Eskimos" example, the problem-solver might immediately appreciate the fact that refrigerators can be used for more than keeping food cold. By maintaining a constant temperature, they can also prevent food from freezing where the ambient temperature is below 32 F. They would seek out people confronted with exactly that challenge and would take pride in helping them solve the problem.

But what if you learned your line of refrigerators started fires in several homes due to faulty electrical components? Would you still want to sell it to a customer? Or what if your product is known to be damaging to the user? Twenty years ago, there were mixed messages on tobacco products, but today cigarettes are known to be hazardous to health. If you worked for a large tobacco company, how would you feel about promoting the product? What about asbestos products? Or breast implants, or intrauterine birth control devices with a known high failure rate? What if you knew your product was damaging to the environment? Would you sell an addictive drug like cocaine if it were legal?

Of course, there are people actively selling products today that are known to be harmful or illegal. They justify their actions in many ways. As human beings, our most developed skill may be self-justification. We act first and then defend our actions.

You have undoubtedly heard, and maybe even used, some of the more common defenses for these choices. For example: "Somebody's gonna make a profit—it might as well be me." The argument that someone is going to sell it anyway is often put forth to justify participation. There will always be someone providing drugs or prostitutes or (fill in the blank). The self-justifying seller tells himself that at least he makes sure his are pure, clean, and so on.

When I was a teenager, my mother often challenged, "If everyone's jumping in the lake, does that mean you have to?" Far more concerned with peer approval than catching pneumonia, I always answered, "Sure! Why not?" Once I became a parent myself, I saw it differently. I became aware of the many potential dangers, both real and imagined, threatening my child if she jumped in a lake: pneumonia or frostbite, of course, since I lived in Wisconsin, but also riptides, sharp rocks, cramps, fast boats, carnivorous fish, and sea serpents … you get the idea.

As adults, we have a responsibility to lead, not merely to follow. We have a duty to ourselves, our children, and our fellow citizens in this world to evaluate our choices and understand their consequences. "Everybody's doing it" may make it easier to abdicate our responsibility, but it won't make it right. When we fail to align our behavior with our principles, we suffer the consequences of stress. We experience "Maalox® moments," the result of our bodies and our souls being out of harmony. And the "lesser of two evils" justification, arguing that our product may be harmful but at least it's not as bad as the product that less-ethical people sell, carries no weight. Having the purest cocaine or the most hygienic needles doesn't alter the fact that the product ultimately addicts and destroys its users.

Another popular rationalization is that everybody has personal choice, including the right to destroy themselves should they so choose. Most of us learn through sad personal experience that we are powerless to prevent someone we care about from harming herself if she is determined to do so, but that does not give us the right to make the tools of destruction easily accessible. In any philosophical debate on free choice, contradictions are quick to appear. For example, many people who oppose abortion as murder support capital punishment with clear consciences. People who defend their right to smoke cigarettes and breathe their sidestream smoke into a public place may abhor the law that allows medically assisted suicide in Oregon. People who argue for their right to consume alcohol without limits may consider the legalization of marijuana or other mood-altering drugs to be unthinkable.

My father used to tell a story about the preacher who enthusiastically mounted the podium on Sunday and denounced gambling. A little old lady in the front row joined in with, "Amen, Brother." Then he denounced smoking. Again she cried, "Amen, Brother." When he denounced drinking, she stood up and walked out, muttering, "Hmph. Now he's done quit preachin' and started in meddlin'."

When I was a smoker and a fervent defender of my individual right to smoke, I could have represented a tobacco company as a sales professional with no feeling of conflict. Today I understand more about addiction and would be challenged by my awareness that once addiction takes hold, the concept of choice is meaningless. If I sold an addictive substance, I would be defending or justifying my own choice at the expense of others. The old saying "misery loves company" may be true, but it doesn't give me permission to hand out misery like party invitations so that I won't have to suffer alone.

Selling with soul challenges us to be consistent, to align our principles with our behavior. People who sold cigarettes or asbestos ceiling tile twenty years ago did not know about carcinogens. We are not prescient, nor do we have the ability to predict what scientific research may yet reveal. As salespeople, however, we are recommending products and are responsible for staying informed and knowledgeable about them. We learn the product as well as the many ways it can be applied, recognizing that a safe product can be used in unsafe ways. When we learn of safety hazards or misuse of products, we inform our customers and make sure they know how not to make the same error.

It can be painful to have a purchase order in hand, the one you have worked six months or more to earn, only to discover that the cabling for your product is not suitable for plenum and will not meet the life safety requirements of your semiconductor-manufacturing customer. For a moment or two, we might all be tempted to close our eyes and cover our ears while singing "na na na" at the top of our lungs. Unfortunately, in addition to looking silly, we would then become part of the problem rather than part of the solution. Integrity demands full disclosure.

The Iroquois nation made no decisions before asking themselves what the effect would be on the seventh generation to follow. This kind of long-term thinking is foreign to us today, when everything moves at lightning speed and the pressure to act and move on is unrelenting. The process itself is best understood by example.

I recently planted six rosebushes in my backyard and was told by the nursery to be sure to use a broad-spectrum insecticide to prevent disease. My neighbor is an organic gardener and would be appalled if I chose to use toxic chemicals in my adjoining land. Now, I may believe strongly in my right to use chemicals on my rosebushes on my own land even though fences don't prevent soil from my yard from being blown off or drained off onto my neighbor's land. And if I needed to sell my property and had to increase its curb appeal in order to sell quickly and at maximum profit, the idea of quick-acting chemicals with guaranteed results would be even easier to justify. Whoever bought my house could negotiate with my neighbor themselves long after I had moved on. But there is more to consider.

If my house sat on my dream property with water frontage, those chemicals are likely to work their way into the water through runoff. My six little rosebushes might not be the equivalent of the *Exxon Valdez*, but what if the toxic chemicals poisoned the food supply for the fish? Or contributed to the growth of algae that choked the life out of the river downstream? Can I easily defer that problem to the person who purchases my property?

What if I learned the purchaser was going to be my own daughter? Or that my grandson would be playing and swimming in that very stream ten years from now? How would this knowledge affect my decision?

The more we consider the long-term effects of our decisions, the more difficult it becomes to weigh the various factors. Yet when businesses fail to be responsible community citizens, many critics blame short-term thinking. Many decisions appear to be driven by shareholders' demands for a favorable quarterly report. Stock traders may sell off or divest businesses at the first missed revenue forecast, rather than taking the long view.

When decisions are driven by the hurdle rate or ROI (return on investment) or other ratios, it is difficult to justify investments with "soft" returns, such as community service or public education. A local elementary school may someday supply employees back to the business, but there is no guarantee and the students are many years away from providing a measurable "return."

In the early 1990s, studies were done and projections made on the makeup of the workforce in the year 2000. Analysts agreed that the workforce would be increasingly diverse, with as much as 60 percent of it comprised of women and minorities. Yet this same percentage of the population often makes up an "at risk" group in the schools. Along the road to college and careers, students encounter multiple obstacles and detours, from the lure of unprotected sex and easy access to drugs, to the peer support and surrogate family life of gangs. If this is not seen as a business issue today, it surely will be when we are experiencing firsthand the effects of cutbacks in school funding: a shortfall of engineers and scientists, and the complaints of high-technology companies that they cannot recruit and retain enough talented personnel. If it takes a village to raise a child, what does it take to raise our standards for the businesses within that village?

Efforts to raise funds for community agencies are commendable and always appreciated by the community they serve. But can your company do more? The large, well-publicized fund-raiser is important, but small, day-to-day efforts that build a bridge between business and community are the best at deepening empathy and fostering ongoing support.

Sometimes all it takes is a little initiative on the part of an employee to create a large increase in awareness and involvement. Salespeople with soul are not afraid to lead by example or "to put some skin in the game." They are the ones who organize a team to participate in a charity walk and enjoy a picnic with their families afterward. They are the ones who get a group of homeowners together and volunteer to help Habitat for Humanity or a local housing program. They are the ones who propose the department "adopt a family" or in some other way pitch in and help someone in the community.

In my own experience at the branch office level, all of the above activities have taken place, as well as individual contributions of major impact. One young woman participated in Big Sisters because she remembers it was a mentor who wouldn't let her quit that kept her on track to an engineering degree and a career she loves. Another degreed engineer volunteers his time to teach at-risk high school students about the basics of electricity and motors. Another teaches programming language for industrial controllers. These kids may not have any immediate use for the concepts, but they are intellectually curious and enjoy the challenge. Nothing makes more of a difference in a kid's life than spending time with an adult who is excited about learning. Love of learning, like fire, requires only a small amount of kindling and a spark to take off. Once kids acquire a love of learning, they are less likely to burn out from self-destructive behaviors and more likely to be lit up and on fire with awareness of their own potential.

Change Companies or Become a Change Agent?

When you are committed to taking your soul to work on a daily basis, you must decide whether you will change companies or become a change agent within your present company. These are tougher choices than they first appear.

If you decide to change companies, you face one set of challenges. If all your life you've sold tobacco products, for example, you may have a difficult time convincing a company that sells vitamins or footwear or another line that your skills are transferable. Although some sales trainers will argue that if you can sell one thing, you can sell anything, many employers are not convinced. If you have examined your company and found it wanting, examine yourself, taking care to identify your skills and your assets. This is no time to be humble. Make a list of all your accomplishments. Look at where you succeeded while others failed. Go back through your performance review letters or your initial job references, and remind yourself of what it is about you that has always impressed others. Reaffirm your own value.

This is also the time to ask yourself what you would most like to sell or promote. Are you a waterskiing enthusiast? Has it always been your dream to own a recreational vehicle? Are you enamored of computer technology and longing to be part of that industry? Talk to people in the industry you admire. Find out what they look for, and evaluate what it will take for you to be qualified in their eyes. Don't be afraid to invest in yourself and your future with additional training. As the rate of change accelerates, we are being forced to evolve from a society that only measures what you've already learned in the past to a society dependent on how quickly you learn right now. Salespeople with soul are lifelong learners and recognize the importance of continuous improvement in creating value with their customers.

If you decide to stay and become a change agent within your company, you face a different set of challenges. You will need to use all your best sales skills internally, while realizing you have more on the line than one sale or one customer relationship. Before you begin, prepare yourself mentally and emotionally to leave if necessary. Update your resume. Go on an interview just to make sure you are up-to-date on both your interview ability and your current worth in the market. Remind yourself that you have choices and the right to change your mind. You will be actively lobbying and working for a correction of the situation that has made it difficult for you to feel unqualified pride in your company or product. Perhaps this means working with product marketing toward full disclosure of the product's risks as well as its many features and benefits. Perhaps it means working with product engineering to correct a safety issue. Or perhaps it means working with research and development to find a new product or application that you can represent with pride.

Choose your battle and fight wisely, qualifying the opportunity to lead change the way you would qualify a prospective sale. Ask yourself: Is this a realistic goal? What is the probability I'll succeed? Can I reach the people who can make the decision? Can I explain the benefit of making the change beyond making it a moral issue? Do I have a champion who will sponsor me? What is my fallback position if I fail?

People will respond to your efforts along the full range of human emotions. Some will find you threatening or just annoying, while others will think your point is irrelevant and wonder if you have too much time on your hands. Some will see you as disloyal or as lowering morale. Some will be angry with you for not toeing the line and accuse you of sabotaging the team's efforts. You may be fired or "riffed" in the next reduction in force. The old saw that the squeaky wheel gets the grease ignores the very real threat that the squeaky wheel may just get replaced.

You will find people who are grateful for the information, who strongly agree with you but have no "authority" to solve the problem. And you will wonder many nights if you are Sisyphus, endlessly rolling a rock uphill only to have it relentlessly crash back down. None of these options is easy, and you may find yourself "out of step" to the point of being drummed right out of the band. That's the risk you face, and it carries with it the reality that it is much harder to find a new job when you are unemployed than while you are still working.

Why would anyone choose this road? Because it is essential to our own success and to the long-range success of business that when we find our actions out of line with our principles, we work to bring them back to alignment. Not everyone is willing or able to take on the challenges of ministry or police work or hospice care, but it is easy to see how valuable these jobs are and how much we rely on the people who do them. The task of leading change from within corporate America may be the most difficult of all challenges facing business people today, and yet it is also the most urgent. The late Peter Drucker, writer, professor, and thought leader, wrote in his book *Management Challenges for the 21st Century* that every leader must face the ethical considerations of their decisions. Such questions are as important for ethical considerations as they are for questions of profit and investment.

Another consequence of making this choice is the need to continuously reassess your progress. Corporations, like large ships, turn slowly. Cultural change generates more resistance than any other kind. How will you know you are making a difference? Setting realistic goals and choosing your metrics will be essential to sustaining your commitment and your energy over the long haul. This requires understanding the company and the players, and analyzing correctly who is invested in the status quo and who may be your ally in the effort to lead change. When it comes down to it, this is selling at the highest possible level and all the skills you have acquired and refined to be an effective professional salesperson will be required to achieve your objective. As in all selling, however, the goal will be solving the problem to mutual benefit. In this case, you will benefit from achieving congruence between your principles and those of the company you represent, and the company will benefit from becoming a positive force rather than a harmful one in the future. You will have sold management on its larger mission.

REFLECTIONS ON CHAPTER 3
First, Do No Harm: The Company and Product You Represent

There can be no happiness if the things we believe in are different from the things we do.
—Unknown

Before choosing whether to change companies or to become a change leader within your present company, ask yourself these questions:

1. What is your company's mission statement, and do you agree or disagree with it?

2. Does your company "walk the talk"? Are the messages you get from your manager consistent with the priorities indicated by the mission statement?

3. Is there one change you would make in the day-to-day activities of your office that would help you feel more pride in your company? What can you do to promote that change?

4. Are you proud of your product? Are you satisfied that it is a quality product made for high reliability? Are there safety considerations you need to discuss with your customers? Delivery issues?

5. What is your own personal mission statement?

6. If you were a product being sold, how would you describe your features? The benefits you bring to others?

7. Think about how many hours you spend working or doing work-related activities each day. Divide your total earnings by those hours. Are you investing your time wisely? Are you getting a good return?

8. If you are married or in a committed relationship, would your partner answer these questions differently? Have you discussed your career goals and made sure you both have the same expectations of time and effort required to reach them?

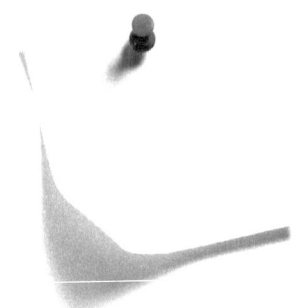

Note to Self: I represent my values, not just my company.

CHAPTER 4

The Matter Of Personal Styles

A COMMITMENT TO ONGOING personal development is essential to the professional salesperson. Continuous learning becomes a way of life for the best of us. Stephen Covey uses a story about Abraham Lincoln to make this point: If your job is to cut down a tree, you need to first make sure your saw is sharp. Each of us is our own "saw," and staying sharp requires attention to more than product, market, and competitive information. It requires us to develop self-knowledge as well.

One often-neglected area of preparation is learning about personal style, both your own and others'. The image of salespeople as extroverts with flashy smiles and a collection of jokes is one more stereotype we need to bury. Professional salespeople come in many styles and personalities. The best, however, have a versatility that allows them to understand and to build empathy with a broad cross section of customers.

When salespeople read articles on the importance of versatility, they sometimes interpret that as trying to be "all things to all people." Sales trainers will tell their students to "mirror" the customer's body language and "paraphrase" the customer's words back to him in order to establish rapport. In fact, few things are more annoying than having someone sitting across from you in a "monkey see, monkey do" stance, and most rookies "parrot" rather than paraphrase. When I try to use a style too far from my own, I sacrifice my authenticity. Customers pick up on my discomfort, and my credibility suffers. There are few things that will call your integrity into doubt as quickly as trying to masquerade as someone you are not.

There is a significant difference between respecting different styles and seeking to imitate them. Step one is learning your own style, or how you act when you're not thinking much about it. Each of us has a comfort zone that we developed over the years. It is comprised of our personalities, our culture, our education, our family and regional influences, and more. Psychologists and sociologists classify these behavior types in various ways. Regardless of the model used, most methods delineate types based on which method of social interaction and decision making we prefer.

The Myers-Briggs model, for example, groups people in the following categories: introvert/extrovert, sensing/intuition, thinking/feeling, and judging/perceiving. Another popular method of style analysis uses color-coding of red, blue, yellow, or white to differentiate between personalities. Yet another model, which I was first introduced to through a Holden Learning course called "S-4," categorizes people as drivers, amiables, expressives, and analyticals. PDP, Inc., uses the four category descriptors dominance, extroversion, pace, and conformity.

While each differs in terminology and method of categorization and some rely on self-assessment while others require input from your peers and coworkers, the differences are less important than what these tools have in common. At an elemental level, they help us to examine whether or not we get energy from other people or find ourselves drained after a prolonged period without time alone. They look at whether we prefer to make decisions based on our "gut feel" or only after reviewing the numbers and data. And they help us understand whether we are most interested in the "big picture" end result or more concerned with the individual steps and details along the way.

If your company does not do personality profiling, I recommend you contact a training company like those mentioned above and have a profile completed, preferably one that provides you with questionnaires for your coworkers or customers to fill out in addition to your self-evaluation. That way you have a good comparison between how you see yourself and how others see you.

The first time I completed a profile, I expected the results to verify that I was an expressive type: a good communicator, friendly, motivated by recognition, outgoing with people, and so on. I was shocked when the questionnaire results from my peers and customers came back depicting me as a solid, dyed-in-the-wool driver, bottom-line focused, impatient with details, showing little emotion other than determination to succeed, and taking little time for relationships. I didn't recognize this person at all!

At the same time, I began to understand why some of the people in my company reacted to me as they did. Gradually I understood that my insecurity about selling, and my fear of failing, were distorting my behavior. I was operating from stress or, as the Holden trainers had put it, my "backup" zone. As the only woman in my branch office, I was also being careful not to act feminine or show any part of my personality that might emphasize how I was different. People were seeing my tension and determination, rather than my true self as I would act in my comfort zone. Years later, after I had achieved success in selling and was confident enough to reveal more of myself to my peers and coworkers, I was retested. The results of that test, and several others since, showed my true expressive nature.

Understanding yourself is a prerequisite to understanding others. The better you know your own nature, the better you can identify where you need to stretch your abilities in order to work well with people representing other styles. The very traits in others that drive you crazy may be the parts of yourself that you deny. Making peace with those parts of yourself, accepting yourself and others in all their wondrous complexity and diversity, is at the heart of spiritual growth and serenity. It is also a prerequisite for selling with soul.

Stereotypes abound regardless of profession. The less experience we have, the more we're convinced that engineers are introverted and detail-minded, chief executive officers are extroverted and big-picture oriented, human resources people are amiable, peacemaking types, and so forth. Salespeople, we all "know," are extroverted, loud back-slappers, armed with bad jokes, relying on their intuition or "gut feel," and bored with details. Yet any group of successful salespeople will include representatives of every type of personality category. They may be studious and introverted. They may be compulsive about details. They may distrust intuition and demand data. What they will all have in common is an understanding of their own style, its strengths and limitations, and a respectful appreciation for the styles of others.

If you are by nature an extrovert, you make decisions best when you can talk them out with other people. Brainstorm. Kick it around. Run it up the flagpole. The risk is that you may only be "tossing it out there," while others hear what you say as a firm position and try to hold you to it.

Or, if you are an extrovert whose ego is out of control, you may become be so enamored of your own ideas that you have trouble hearing anyone else and will single-mindedly focus on persuading others to your views. The flip side is the extrovert whose self-confidence ebbs and flows based on the feedback of people around her. In talking with others, she may be too easily swayed by their opinions.

The learning opportunity is to look at the strengths and the weaknesses of your style. If you are an extrovert calling on another extrovert, the risk is that you may engage in a battle for "airtime" with your customer, finding it hard to listen and analyze. Or, when calling on an introverted customer, you may overpower him or her by freely sharing your opinions and views and failing to draw out his or hers. Developing your listening skills will be vital in your personal development. Balancing your natural instinct to always seek out other people by planning for periods of solitary review and reflection will be important to your spiritual growth.

If you are an introvert, you prefer to make decisions alone and excel at taking action without waiting for a committee to give its blessing. On the other hand, you may find it hard to concentrate when bombarded by other opinions. You may have difficulty in teamwork situations, preferring to go out and get the job done on your own, even if you fail, rather than having to involve a group of other people. Nonetheless, introverts need to seek out additional facts and perspectives. When calling on customers, your natural tendency to "go inside" for energy and information may make it harder for you to comfortably engage in detailed discussions, social conversation, or storytelling with others. Having your questions ready in advance of a sales call will make it much easier for you to draw out the information you need.

If you are a "big-picture" kind of person and easily bored by details, you may excel at helping your customers see the benefits they will realize. Your drive for results may be a strong asset in meeting your goals. However, the risk you face is a tendency to gloss over details. You may make mistakes at the detail level because you hurry through. When your customers press for details, you may procrastinate because you hate "cranking numbers" or doing paperwork. Not satisfying their request in a timely manner, though, shows disrespect to your more detail-minded customer and may cost you some credibility.

If you thrive on details, analyzing everything at least three different ways, you may work well with customers of like style, but you must be certain you understand their priorities so that your analysis and the details you provide are not perceived as irrelevant or overkill. With customers who are only concerned about the bottom line, you may be perceived as boring or wasting their time by providing unnecessary information. Your development will be enhanced by taking time before each meeting to step back and look at the big picture, reminding yourself of your destination, before you get lost in the markings on the road map. Rational thinkers need to stop and check their "gut" from time to time, to feel what their body is telling them about the "facts."

Balance comes from understanding our own areas of weakness and strength. It is only after we have honestly looked in the mirror that we can grasp what our customers need to feel supported and confident in making a decision. It is only then that we can be respectful of their needs, without compromising our own integrity.

REFLECTIONS ON CHAPTER 4
The Matter of Personal Styles

I can't give you a sure-fire formula for success, but I can give you a formula for failure: try to please everybody all the time.
—Herbert Bayard Swope

Answering the questions below may help you clarify your own style and your biases toward one style or the other. Self-awareness is required for us to sell with empathy and integrity.

1. Describe your favorite customer. What is it you like most about him or her?
2. Describe your least-favorite customer. What is it you most dislike?
3. Does your least-favorite customer remind you of anyone from your past with whom you had difficulty?
4. Does your least-favorite customer remind you of qualities in yourself you have worked hard to change or overcome?
5. What adjustments in your own style could you make that would put this least-favorite customer at ease? For example, would providing a spreadsheet analysis of your recommendation help? Or would a quick bulleted summary be more appreciated?
6. In assessing your own strengths and weaknesses, what do you see as an opportunity for you to learn more versatility?

Note to Self: Remember to be myself but to also honor differences.

CHAPTER 5

How People Buy Today

How we buy and sell products today has changed significantly from how we once did it, and such a major change necessitates new behaviors. Today's rate of change, described by Bill Gates as business @ the speed of thought, challenges us to run full speed just to keep pace. Our customers are also being driven by change, as companies demand more productivity from each individual and at the same time eliminate resources on which we've come to rely. To understand selling, it helps to understand buying.

Buying patterns have changed as dramatically over the past twenty years as technology or manufacturing. Taking a look at your own buying patterns can help you understand customer behavior. To stock your pantry shelves and purchase commodity items like toilet paper and laundry detergent, you probably make a trip once a month to a wholesale buying club like Sam's or Costco. You know you will receive a low price in exchange for buying goods in large quantity, navigating large crowds, and doing without bagging. If you are buying fresh produce, bread, and eggs, you stop at the local supermarket sometime over the weekend and buy just enough for the week ahead. Although the prices will be higher than if you bought in bulk, your lower volume of use makes this the economical alternative to waste and spoilage. If you run out of milk on Wednesday and have to buy it in between leaving work and driving the kids to their soccer game, you may forego the local supermarket altogether in favor of a quick stop at the twenty-four-hour convenience store. You know you will pay more for the milk than at the supermarket, but the time you save is more important than the price.

These are all "commodities," products that have many substitutes available and that are used often and completely. Common wisdom dictates that if a product is a "commodity," it is purchased in a simple "transaction" and price will be the driving factor. Notice in your own behavior, however, how ease of doing business, convenience, and product quality can also come into play. How you purchase can result in significant differences in price when other factors like your time and freshness or quality are important to you.

Looking at another example, if you are purchasing blue jeans and T-shirts, you may look no further than Target or K-Mart, where a simple transaction should be attractive due to a low price. If you are purchasing a suit to wear to a job interview or a dress to wear to the boss's son's wedding, you probably will go to Nordstrom or another high-end store known for customer service. You will pay more, but the service and assistance of the salesclerk, possibly even the personal shopper, is valuable to help you purchase an outfit that will provide the additional benefits of confidence and pride in how you look. Many people rely on a salesclerk or personal shopper to call them when products that would match their taste and personal style arrive or go on sale. It's still a clothing purchase, but we have abandoned the simple commodity transaction in favor of a "relationship" or "consultative" purchasing pattern.

So if there is no hard and fast rule about what "drives" a decision, how does a salesperson develop an understanding of a buyer's preferences and behavior pattern? The key is what is often referred to as the value proposition: *The value the customer expects to receive must be equal to or greater than the investment the customer must make.*

Price is a consideration in all purchasing behavior, but it is often not the primary or even one of the top three drivers of the decision to buy. Quality of product, ease of doing business, reliability and service, warranty and training, and trust in the sales representative and the company all come into play, and each buyer will weight these factors differently depending on the current situation. Put another way, the immediate problem the customer is attempting to solve will determine the relative importance of each factor in the buying decision. The investment itself can be money, time, training, risk, or reputation.

Business buyers display a similar range of behaviors and priorities. Some customers are willing to make large investments of money, believing "you get what you pay for." These buyers put great store in a recognizable or premium brand and consider the company infrastructure behind the product to be part of the package. They are less willing to make high-risk purchases just to save money and often have less time to investigate alternatives to what they perceive to be the leading brand. Even at the consumer level, lines form for iPhones at each release, and we pay higher prices for them, ignoring the claims of other smartphones to offer lower cost, superior speed, or other advantages.

Other business buyers prefer to save money and will invest large amounts of time considering alternatives to the brand leader. They may even consider the education they receive while investigating alternate approaches to be part of the benefit received. Linux and open systems running on minicomputers from now-defunct companies were popular choices with university and technical buyers who took pride in being immune to the market power of "Big Blue" and were confident that they had the intellectual resources to take another approach that would save money. They did not value the support staff of the vendor and believed they could not only implement the system themselves, but develop innovations and enhancements to it.

Some buyers prefer to take risk and be the pioneers in their industries. They delight in being in the forefront of what is jokingly called the bleeding edge of technology. Geoffrey Moore, in his book *Inside the Tornado*, labels them early adopters. Often they are willing to pay more and will buy "serial #1" of a new product just to be able to say they are the first to have it.

The salesperson with soul takes time to learn the customer's preferred buying pattern for a specific project and does not generalize or stereotype the customer's behavior across the board. Although our basic personalities may not change, our behaviors do, as we tackle different problems and face different choices. Our customers, too, vary in their actions and choices.

Selling with soul is facilitating a customer's problem solving for mutual benefit. Every sales call and every interaction should be preceded by asking yourself two questions:

- What am I going to do for you?
- What are you going to do for me?

Understand the problem, understand how the customer weights the various factors that affect the buying decision, and make certain the benefit received is equal to or greater than the investment you seek. That is creating value for your customer.

Many salespeople believe their job is to find out what the customers value and then communicate to them how their product or service delivers it. If all you are to your customer is a walking, talking advertisement, however, is it worth their time to see you? If the buyer wants a summary of the value provided by your product, he or she can peruse your catalog, read a brochure, visit your website, or talk to another user. Many of these activities take less time and are accomplished with less stress than scheduling meetings with salespeople. In fact, John Holland, in his excellent book *Rethinking the Sales Cycle*, points out that many buyers today are already well along in their buying decision before they even talk to a salesperson.

He says, "The buyer is now able to gather all the technical and commercial information they want on any vendor, any product, and many applications. Because the stereotype of sales people in our culture leads to buyers wanting to avoid us, many prospective customers today do all of the first phase of buying on their own. They gather data, they build a list of requirements, they form opinions and rank possible solutions, often before a salesperson is even allowed to participate in the process. (p.76)"

If salespeople are just communicating value, they are significantly overpaid. Salespeople must *create* value for the customer. To test yourself and your skill at this part of your job, ask yourself some hard questions:

1. What information can I provide this customer that a brochure cannot?
2. Can I supply details that are unique or particular to this customer's application or environment?
3. Can I provide information gleaned from other users that show how the product is best applied?
4. Can I demonstrate this product more effectively for this customer than our website can?
5. Have I prepared myself thoroughly so that any time this customer spends with me will be efficient and rewarding for him or her?

Mediocre salespeople can easily and economically be replaced by technology. The true professional, on the other hand, always has job security because both his employer and his customers can identify the value he creates in the exchange. The investment made always matches or exceeds the value received.

Many salespeople think their "relationship" is what adds value.

"I've known Jack for years! He'd never think of buying from anyone else."

"Sue and I are friends. We go out to dinner with her and her husband."

"Bill would never let me down."

In the words of the movie *The Godfather*, this is "nothing personal. It's business."

It's a wonderful experience to form friendships with our business contacts. Life is short, and the more we laugh and share with others, the richer it feels. But just as a husband and wife can vote for different candidates, eat different foods, and still stay married, keeping your friendship intact should not depend on your customer buying from a buddy. The customer is paid to solve the business problem efficiently and effectively, and today there are more purchasing options than ever before.

When your buddy Ben needs to purchase commodities or replacements, he expects a simple transaction. Price is known. There's no haggling. And there are no complicated choices to be made about extras. You might be his oldest friend in the world, but remember: value received must be equal to or greater than the investment made. Ben will be justifiably upset if you drag your personal friendship into an exchange he needs to keep as efficient and price-effective as possible.

Put yourself in Ben's shoes: You drive up to a McDonald's window expecting to get a lunch for under three dollars and in less than three minutes. Imagine your surprise when your next-door neighbor pokes her head out the service window. Now, you genuinely like this person. She's brought soup over when you had the flu. Taken in your mail when you were out of town. Taken your surplus zucchinis in the fall. But you are at a McDonald's and already late to get back to the office. Before filling your order, the friendly person behind the counter smiles and starts a conversation, asking you questions like, "Are you on your lunch break? How's the job going? How's your family? Seen any good movies lately?" Chances are good your blood pressure will begin to rise and you will swear never to stop at that McD's again. Value expected did not match value received. Most of us would prefer an efficient if garbled voice coming out of a clown's mouth if it meant we'd get our bag of food and our change *fast*.

Our customers feel the same way when they are making simple commodity purchases. The salesperson with soul understands that and, rather than investing time in small talk or trying to form a friendship, invests time in teaching the customer the most efficient ways to make the exchange. There are many more buying resources today, and just the wide range of choices can be baffling to your customer. The salesperson with soul takes the time to help the customer sort it out. For example:

1. Help the customer log onto your *website* and show her how to use the online catalog. If demonstrations of products or detailed specifications are available online, show her how to access these as well.
2. Set your customer up to use your company's electronic purchasing or e-commerce site.
3. If your customer relies on printed materials, spend ten minutes giving him an overview of the most recent printed catalog. Highlight and clip the sections covering products he routinely purchases.
4. Preprint order forms for products the customer routinely buys and highlight key boxes.
5. Help your customer set up an account and line of credit with your 1-800-number, so she can do routine purchasing with a minimum of paperwork.
6. If getting quick answers to product questions is part of getting the order right, introduce your customer to an individual from the inside sales staff that he can come to depend on.
7. Train, train, train.

The best tools in the world are no good unless the person using them is competent and comfortable. While you may believe your website or catalog to be "intuitively obvious" or your business system "idiot-proofed," people outside your company may find them intimidating. By helping your customer learn how to use the resources with confidence, you create value despite the fact that the purchases will be simple transactions.

At the opposite end of the spectrum are complex sales, which often call for an ongoing consultative relationship. In this type of selling, fully understanding the customer's business problem on all levels is prerequisite to success. The chapter "Qualifying: Respecting Yourself and Your Customer" provides detailed discussion of how to get the information needed to be a good consultant and business partner.

Many large companies over the past several years have written contracts with one supplier for a wide array of products and services. From janitorial supplies to electric lighting, pipe, and wire, they want one "integrated supplier" to process the transaction, source the materials from the best-priced supplier, package and deliver the goods, and generate one invoice for the transaction. In addition to this service, they expect to receive a variety of reports on their purchases, supporting documentation on how much time and money they have saved, and recommendations for how to secure additional cost reduction or improved service.

In such an arrangement, the individual salesperson representing each of the product lines, or the distributor formerly relied on for all electrical products, are viewed as superfluous. If the salesperson is considered an unnecessary middleman, the customer will want to bypass him or her and deal directly with the factory. The underlying assumption many of us make is that eliminating the middleman eliminates costs and should result in a lower price. So many students taking their first marketing class have had this axiom drummed into them that it is often unquestioned. But as many of us have learned the hard way from seeing the people who used to perform specific tasks in our companies downsized out of a job, you can eliminate the *person*, but not the function the person performed, unless you reengineer the process itself.

If the customer has relied on the salesperson to help her select product, as well as to hold her hand and train her people once the product is delivered, someone must be identified to provide that aftermarket service. If the manufacturer has always relied on distributors for entering orders, stocking and delivering product, and invoicing the customer, the manufacturer will have to create a whole new infrastructure to take these functions back in-house and do them efficiently. In fact, the efficiencies the manufacturer gained by outsourcing these functions may mean the customer is paying less for product through a distributor than if he or she bought it directly. The professional salesperson must know what value he or she adds and be able to clearly articulate that to the customer. A professional who is not able to do so is an endangered species.

Whether we are talking about transactions, complex sales, or national contracts for integrated supply, people remain responsible for making it all work. Professional salespeople continue to be valued precisely because there is no better way to perform their most vital function: problem solving for mutual benefit.

REFLECTIONS ON CHAPTER 5
How People Buy Today

No computer network with pretty graphics can ever replace the salespeople that make our society work.
—Clifford Stoll

It is a challenge to stay current on technology, new product launches, and changes in your business as well as your customer's business. Change is constant, and to sell with soul we have to embrace it. Ask yourself the questions below and think about your answers. What new learning or new direction do your answers point you toward?

1. Have you kept up with the technology available to you to help your customers? Do you resist changes to how business is done?
2. Do you ask yourself before each customer contact what you will do for him in this meeting and what you will ask him to do for you?
3. Are you giving a quote before learning what the customer really wants and needs? Are you trying to get price out there early so you can "close"? Have you taken the time to really understand what your customer needs to achieve the result she wants?
4. Do you see the customer as having all the power and knowledge and forget that you are a knowledgeable professional yourself?

Figure 3. Don't give away your power. You and the customer are both professionals, each with your own knowledge and skills.

CHAPTER 6

Sales Basics

SELLING, AS PROBLEM SOLVING, is completing a series of steps, and this is true whether you represent a product or service that is often purchased in one sales call or you represent a complex project or product offering that requires you to complete these steps over a period of six to eighteen months.

The first step is called prospecting or *new business development* and involves finding potential buyers. This aspect of selling is so important that many sales managers create specialist positions to do just this. They are called *hunters*, and the people who take over the day-to-day business of a new account once the first sale has been completed are often referred to as *gatherers* or *farmers*. The best prospectors are also highly skilled in step two, qualifying the opportunity.

Qualifying, or as Neil Rackham's SPIN model of selling puts it, *investigation*, is the step of gathering information on your prospective buyer, starting with the general situation today, the business needs or goals the customer must address, and the obstacles to meeting them successfully. Many of us were taught that qualifying an opportunity meant getting the answers to the big three: Who is the decision maker? Do you have the budget? Are you ready to buy? At the heart of those questions is the main stereotype of a seller's thinking: "What's in this for *me*?" A better approach is to learn as much as you can about the customer, the business, the problem, the potential ways to solve the problem, the obstacles to implementing a solution, and the time frame in which your solution will be evaluated. Asking good questions and listening fully to the answers is the most important tool in selling.

Presentation or Proposal refers to the step in which you present the solution you and the customer have agreed best helps him solve his problem, the benefits he has said he will enjoy after implementing the proposed solution, and the value of moving forward. This phase of the selling process is the one most people think of when they think of salespeople as being "good talkers." However, if you have done the second stage, qualifying, effectively, the presentation becomes a summary and a discussion of what you have learned—what the customer has agreed will help—and an opportunity for the customer to confirm it.

An old rule in sales is that it's best to demonstrate your product before the other competitors show theirs and then try to get the "last look" as well just before the customer makes the decision. The truth is that a demonstration done early is often a deal killer. If you haven't taken the time to understand what the customer really wants and needs, the demo will be a canned presentation showing everything there is to show about your product. The customer's eyes will glaze over, and she is likely to say, "That's too complicated for us" or "That's way more than we need" and she'll mentally move on to the next vendor. Take the time to do it right—as proof, not as a "spray and pray" sales pitch.

Identifying and responding to objections, often called *overcoming objections*, is really a test of how well you did the previous steps. The solution you have proposed should not hold any surprises for the customer. It should not leave unanswered questions. If serious concerns arise at this point, it is usually an indication that you failed to fully complete an earlier step, either missing key needs or failing to show value.

Closing is the step that has sold hundreds of books. It is the stuff of legends. Everyone has heard of the super closers who never lose a sale. Many of us have been taught formulas and scripts designed to keep the customer from being able to say no. This is all bunk. The stage of the sales cycle known as *closing* should really be nothing more than confirmation of what has gone before and, when done professionally, is a brief blip on the screen before you shift into follow-up and implementation.

Skipping Steps—Do Them Now or Do Them Later

None of the steps can be skipped, because each is essential to making certain you and your customer share a mutual understanding of the problem, its solution, and its implementation, and that your expectations are congruent.

There are many ways to make sure you haven't missed important steps, but the easiest is the sales action plan. Such a plan starts with a simple statement of the problem to be solved, and then goes on to list the steps that will be necessary to identify and implement the best solution. It can be in a complicated project management format, or something as simple as the form that follows this chapter. The important thing is to find a method that works for you and then to work it.

Remember: The only test that matters in evaluating whether or not you have developed a good sales plan and worked it effectively is whether or not, at the end of it, you have a satisfied customer.

The test question to ask after developing a sales action plan is simple: If I complete each of these steps thoroughly and on time, will I help the customer solve his or her problem and earn the business? If you can't answer a firm "yes," go back and ask yourself what steps you forgot or failed to list.

At the end of this chapter is a sample sales action plan that I've used for years. I call it the mini opportunity plan because it fits on one page, no more, and the key elements are the problem or goal and the series of steps the customer and I have to take together to accomplish it. Some of the things that might be included are:

- Meet with each member of the buying/evaluation committee.
- Provide proof of the proposed solution (demo? references? etc.).
- Get legal approval of all necessary documents, terms and conditions, etc.
- Set a timeline for the implementation.
- Agree on expectations and how we will measure the success of the project.

The importance of listing who will do each step, or who is primarily responsible for seeing that it gets done, and the date by which that will happen, cannot be overstated. When a customer buys into the plan and shares responsibility for the success of the project, you have a committed prospect and a high likelihood of success. When all the tasks and obligations are carried by the sales rep alone and the customer's only task is to raise each hoop higher to see if the sales rep can jump through it, you have done a poor job of aligning with the customer's goals and needs and establishing that he, not you, owns the problem and must own the ultimate solution.

    The sales plan, whether it is handwritten on a yellow legal pad, carried in your smartphone, or entered into an elaborate CRM system, is the best way to make sure you haven't skipped steps, you and the customer continue to be aligned, and you will not panic or become reactive as the necessary time and steps are completed. Without a plan, you are a traveler without a map. You may be working hard and running fast, but just where is it you're going?

OPPORTUNITY ACTION PLAN

ACCOUNT _____

ADDRESS _____

_____

CONTACT _____

PHONE _____

E-MAIL _____

ADDITIONAL BUYING INFLUENCES:

_____
_____
_____
_____
_____

PROBLEM / GOAL: _____

_____
_____

TARGET DATE FOR COMPLETION: _____

WHAT TO DO: WHO DOES IT: BY WHEN:

_____
_____
_____
_____
_____
_____
_____
_____

REFLECTIONS ON CHAPTER 6
Sales Basics

He who every morning plans the transaction of the day and follows out that plan, carries a thread that will guide him through the maze of the most busy life. But where no plan is laid, where the disposal of time is surrendered merely to the chance of incidence, chaos will soon reign.
—Victor Hugo

Take some time to reflect on your own experience in selling or being sold to in order to develop more empathy for your buyers.

1. Ask yourself how you like to buy. Do you daydream and look at catalogs? Do you gather data? At which point do you actually talk to a salesperson?
2. When a salesperson asks if she can help you, do you say, "just looking"? Is it because you don't think she can help you? Are you afraid of being "sold" instead of being helped to buy what you want?
3. Are you impatient with others as they work through their decision-making process? Do you want to push them along? Do you see more resistance when you do push them?

Figure 2. I help the customer create a picture of the solution by putting the pieces together one step at a time.

CHAPTER 7
Getting The First Appointment

WHY SHOULD ANYONE IN today's hectic business environment take the time to talk with a sales representative? Many of us today are doing the work formerly done by two people, and trying to put a positive spin on it by calling it "job enrichment." Add to that the accumulated customer resistance due to past experiences with bad salespeople who talk, talk, talk. Every unprofessional sales representative that came before you has made the job of getting the first appointment tougher. How do you differentiate yourself and increase the likelihood that you will get to meet face-to-face with your prospect?

Nearly all salespeople hate prospecting. As soon as they have a good customer base and are making a comfortable income, they put it off with the excuse that they are much too busy taking care of their customers, resolving problems, or doing any other activity that sounds reasonable. Yet prospecting is essential to a healthy business.

The term for finding new opportunities to do business, *prospecting*, brings to mind turning over shovels of dirt looking for a nugget of gold. And the image in many ways is appropriate. But instead of turning over "dirt," your first task in prospecting is turning over piles and piles of data, searching for the nugget of usable information. Just as the prospector seeks the location of a vein that will produce a steady stream of gold, the sales professional seeks a business relationship that will produce a steady stream of opportunities for mutual benefit.

Most salespeople I've worked with hate prospecting to the point where they will avoid it in favor of almost anything, including cleaning out the cat box or having a root canal. We are jealous of the salespeople with the great account, lots of leads, or a good territory. We tell ourselves if only we had a similar setup, we'd have opportunities falling our way. There is an old sales term, *bluebird*, for an opportunity that just drops into your lap. Sounds good, right? Unfortunately, most "bluebirds" need a lot more care and feeding than you ever imagined and inevitably poop on your new pants. I love the following quote from French author Charles Victor Cherbuliez: "What helps luck is a habit of watching for opportunities, of having a patient, but restless mind, of sacrificing one's ease or vanity, of uniting a love of detail to foresight, and of passing through hard times bravely and cheerfully."

The best opportunities are the ones you find yourself and thoroughly qualify. So what keeps us from making the call or writing the letter? The salespeople I work with agree: When you are prospecting, you are just another seller, subject to the stereotypes and negative attitudes many people have about sales—stereotypes that even we may still carry inside us, allowing them to sap our confidence and erode our personal power. Once we have a customer, we look forward to seeing him because we know that in his mind we are differentiated from the stereotype. He knows us and respects us. Why risk all that negativity and rejection we are afraid of getting from prospects? The answer is simple: Without a prospect, no sale is possible.

We need to remind ourselves that there are people out there who need what we provide. They need our knowledge, our products and services, and our commitment to professionalism. And then we need to just do it. If we do nothing, we lose a certain percentage of our installed base every year due to people leaving, companies moving or closing their doors, mergers and acquisitions, and industry cycles. If prospecting is not an option, how do we accomplish the goal of finding more customers in a way that is consistent with selling with soul? How do we maintain Bob's balance when we are already up to our ears in customer issues, deadlines, and other urgent activities? Bob would be the first one to tell you that you will never *find* time to prospect. You have to *make* time to prospect. And he would remind us of the obvious: never put off what is important for the sake of what seems urgent. I contend that prospecting is both important and urgent. We need to make special space for it in our plans, space that is sacred and not subject to being sacrificed for other tasks, and we can do it with integrity and empathy.

Prospecting is an area of sales where many of the old rules and tools no longer apply. E-mail, voice mail, texting, LinkedIn, Facebook, and other technologies have changed how we do it but not why.

There are many people who lament the loss of etiquette and sensitivity in our business and personal lives, observing that many of us no longer take time to perform the little niceties that were once expected of educated professionals. Yet none of us is too busy to appreciate these gracious touches when we see them. The best example of bad manners, disguised as a "skill" in selling, is the "cold call." Many sales training programs still require their trainees to complete a specific number of cold calls before they are considered "qualified" to be sales representatives.

What is a cold call, besides being one of the most disliked activities ever asked of a professional? My favorite definition is from the authors of *Guerrilla Selling*: "They're called 'cold' calls because of the shiver that runs up your spine every time you have to make one." A cold call is walking in without an appointment and asking to see "whoever buys your (fill in your product or service type)." The first person you encounter, if you encounter a person at all, is usually a receptionist who is charged with two principal duties: to represent his or her company in a friendly, professional manner that makes people who call or visit feel welcome, and to screen callers and visitors as effectively as possible, to make sure the management of the company are not distracted, annoyed, or kept from performing their vital functions by any one of the hordes of time-wasters trying to get beyond the gates.

By showing up without an appointment and asking to be let in to see someone, you have just put yourself in the category of time-wasters; and the receptionist must now make every effort to turn you away, without violating the first charter of being friendly and professional. While you may have a wonderful solution to offer someone at that company, you have just created a very real problem for at least one person working there. For this reason, many companies no longer have a front desk except at their main offices. The friendly face has been replaced by a security person or a wall phone that requires you to know your party's extension in order to gain admittance.

Working the cold call from the telephone is similar. Some sales trainers recommend tricks like pretending you and the prospect are good friends. Do they honestly believe most assistants are fooled by this approach? Another suggestion is that you avoid a direct response to a receptionist's screen by changing tacks:

"I hope this won't take long. I'm calling long distance."

"How's his golf game been? Is he in a good mood?"

"I'm about to get on a plane and he won't be able to call me back. I know he'll be upset he missed my call."

Now, if the receptionist puts your call through, she faces the wrath of her boss for being fooled by your sneaky approach. Next time she hears your name, you can count on being blocked completely. Further, her boss will be angry that he and his assistant have been taken in, and you will start off on the wrong foot no matter how right your product might be for this company.

Selling with soul begins with prospecting with integrity and empathy. It requires that we put ourselves in our prospect's shoes and treat her the way we would like to be treated. That means we respect her time, lead with business issues, and be honest about the fact that we are hoping to do business with her.

Reaching voice mail is an opportunity to leave the same message you would have used as an introduction. Providing your name and a brief statement that you have helped other companies in the industry solve problems, followed by the fact that you would like to do the same with this prospect, is sufficient. Don't leave your number and hope he will call back. He won't. You are the one with the responsibility for seeing this communication through to an appropriate conclusion. You can say that you will call him or her "on Tuesday at 9:00 a.m. to request a brief appointment," even though you don't know if 9:00 a.m. on Tuesday is a good time for him. There are two key messages here: The first is that you are specific and committed, and the second is that you keep your commitments.

When you actually do call on Tuesday at 9:00 a.m. to request an appointment, you will have already differentiated yourself from the common herd of people who say they are going to do something but never actually do it. Complaints abound about sales representatives who commit to a phone call or another follow-up action and either don't do it at all or only do it after the customer repeatedly reminds them. By leaving a message and then actually following up, you have shown, "I, too, am a professional, and I have respect for both your time and mine" and you have shown that you keep your word by calling on the appointed day. Whether you connect with the buyer on Tuesday or just with his or her voice mail or assistant, you will leave a message, and you will have earned the right to call again on Wednesday.

If your phone calls do not get you the appointment you seek, write your prospect a note expressing again your desire to meet him or her and to see if there is potential for you to do business together. Enclose your card. Suggest that since this is a very busy time for him, you will contact him again in three weeks, on Thursday, May 17, in the morning and hope he will be able to schedule you for a brief meeting at his convenience. Mark your calendar and make absolutely certain you call him Thursday, May 17, in the morning as promised. As always, being specific and then doing what you say you will do differentiates you from the countless number of vague people who fail to commit and forget to follow up.

Since few people write notes anymore, a handwritten note or letter can stand out. As a fledgling sales representative in the computer industry, I was often given the accounts that met one or more of the following criteria: 1) They had never bought our product; 2) They had strong loyalty to our competitor; and 3) They had thrown out at least three of my predecessors in the recent past. It could have been worse. The president of my company might have run over their puppy dog on their child's fifth birthday; but even without a personal tragedy, they were not favorably disposed toward my company, my products, or me. One breakthrough came from a writing campaign.

The president of the division was a former IBM salesman known to be loyal to his former employer. He, of course, refused to give me an appointment. I began dropping him a note every two weeks, usually handwritten and attached to a copy of a recent article from *Harvard Business Review* or *Computer World* or another respected business source. In the meantime, I continued to telephone or visit the managers who I hoped would become my users. After three months of this campaign, I had almost lost hope, when the IT manager called me and said, "He wants you here Thursday morning to give a presentation to our committee. Can you make it?" Could I make it? I would have crawled through broken glass to be there. What in the world had finally gotten his attention?

The morning of the presentation, the six members of the committee assembled. Each seemed nervous. I'd come to understand that he usually had that effect on people. I set up my materials and waited. And waited. Finally, twenty-five minutes late, Mr. Knudsen swept into the room as though he'd been running a sprint. The breeze from his entry rattled papers all over the table. He pulled out a chair and sat down, saying nothing.

I picked up my business card, swallowed hard, and walked up to him with my hand extended. "I'm Sharon Parker," I started to say, but he cut me off at once.

"I know who you are. I get more mail from you than from my own mother. Show me what you've got."

Everyone laughed, including me. I went through my summary of what I'd learned, and he nodded at each major point.

"You've done your homework. Now what do you think you can do for us that IBM can't?"

Thanks to thorough preparation, I was able to meet that challenge head-on, and two weeks later accepted the first purchase order for a pilot transaction processing system. That bank became my largest account, and although I never saw Knudsen face-to-face again, his data processing manager confided to me later that I had won his respect and his curiosity and he felt he owed it to me and to the bank to listen to what I had to say. As a result, we both benefited.

And, of course, I sent him a thank you note after the meeting. And a letter two weeks later summarizing my discussions with his staff to put together a tailored system for their pilot and the support services they would need for an efficient implementation. But you get the idea …

Today's variations on this technique include e-mail, letters delivered by FedEx or a courier to set them apart, and invitations to a WebEx or to an executive-level seminar. There are many ways to "touch" a customer, and the most successful prospectors are creative, mixing up the media and the message, and using repetition to break through. One of my clients, a very progressive and successful electrical distributor, uses a sequence that includes calls, mail, e-mails, and events to reach new prospects. The point remains the same: When the prospect is worth it, patience and persistence are the required elements to earn the opportunity to sell with soul.

Prepare to Prospect

There is an old saw that defines success as preparation meeting luck. How do you prepare to prospect to maximize your opportunities for success?

First, you must put together a list of prospects to approach. These are companies you have reason to believe can benefit from your product or service. Your prospect list starts with defining your ideal customer by size, industry, processes, or other criteria you choose. You can leverage electronic databases like Dun & Bradstreet, Hoovers, Harris, and so on, or you may want to look at prospecting software such as GoldMine® or Sales Genie® for your own computer or mobile phone. The cost varies by the amount of geography included (one state, two states, the entire United States) and the amount of contact information provided. If purchasing one is out of the question, check your public library to see if they have an online resource. With any database, the information you get out is only as good as what was entered in the first place; and there are always companies that choose not to report or be listed. Consider the results of your search a starting point. Once you have generated your own list, update it regularly with information from the local business section of the newspaper or statewide business publications.

If you have a list of companies you would like to do business with, it is time to fill in the information you will need to successfully contact them. Visiting the prospect company's website can give you contact information, management names and titles, mission statement, whether the company is in growth or expansion mode or a period of cutting back, and other information that will help you form a picture of the company and its culture. So now that we have the who, we move on to what.

Even veteran salespeople often forget the most up-to-date source of information on how your products and services solve problems. Customers are wonderful sources of feedback and detailed information on your product and your company's track record for service. My best education came at the "school of hard knocks," with my customers as faculty. Schedule an interview with some of your best customers and ask essential questions that will help you be a good problem solver in the future. They'll tell you things you won't find on your website or in your literature. For example:

- How long have you been using our product?
- What do you like best about it? What would you change about it if you could?
- Has our company met your expectations?
- How has our service been?
- What could we do to serve you better?
- Who else supplies you with similar products? How do we compare?

You can also use this opportunity to ask the customers general questions about future plans for expansion or consolidation, or more personal questions, like what goals they are working on for this fiscal year, how long they have been with the company, and where they worked before this position. When you hear complaints, don't step into the role of fixer. Be clear that you are seeking feedback that you will communicate within your company, but that you do not control design and engineering. Customer preferences often conflict. State clearly that you are not offering any kind of guarantee that their evaluation will lead to a change in the product. Tell them, though, that they are helping you deepen your understanding of the product, and that this will allow you to better assess where it may and may not solve problems for them in the future.

Existing customers can provide a rich vein of information that is pure gold to the sales professional who takes the time to mine it. For example, only an installed customer can tell you how your product may differ significantly from the features touted in your company's promotional material or about features that don't work quite as advertised. Your installed base of customers is not just a source of information and feedback about your product. It is the best school for you to gain understanding of the problems they face every day, the applications that make or lose money for their companies, and how you can be of service to them.

Too often, sales representatives have only a superficial knowledge of the companies they visit. They may not recognize the difference between a critical process that, if failed, can shut down operations, and a secondary process that can be used as a work buffer during times of varying demand. It's not always obvious to an outsider. For example, if a semiconductor fabrication facility loses power, every chip in process becomes "scrap" and the lost production can cost a million dollars or more. What is the cost of a burned batch of potato chips? Or having to reprint a magazine run because equipment failed to align?

Customers can also tell you how they make purchasing decisions and what their buying process entails. What is most important to them? What is their biggest obstacle? Who do they rely on within the company before making a significant capital decision? What are the organizational interconnections that must be kept healthy?

Another ready source of information that many veteran salespeople forget or do not make time to keep current on is your own product literature. I'm not suggesting you believe everything you read—far from it. Take time to thoroughly reread your sales literature to determine who the brochures are written for: financial and accounting people, buyers and other purchasing professionals, sales and marketing people, engineers and technicians? Who does your company's marketing department think is most likely to purchase your product? What examples are provided? Do they describe where the product has been used? Are references included? Do the claims match what you learned from your customers? It is not enough to know your product's advertised features and benefits; you must become knowledgeable about how it is actually used by customers to solve real business problems.

Similarly, your company's website can provide more than product updates or line card data. The best websites provide online demonstrations, application stories, news items, and market information, all of which can be used as selling tools. The more adept you are at using the website and the more knowledgeable you are of its contents, the more effective you will be at educating your prospective customers.

Some competitive analysis can also be helpful in determining your best prospects. Log onto your competitors' websites and see what they are promoting. What is their vision, their market strategy, their lead product? Request literature. Pay attention to scheduled events or promotions. Some sales representatives make their primary target the largest, best-known company in their area, the one that gets a lot of press and attention, and dream of the day they finally "crack" it. This elephant-hunter mentality can lead to a career-making success story, but in most cases, it results in wasted time and effort. The installed competitor will expend maximum resources to stay installed, and every would-be vendor will do any and everything to break in.

How do you find the opportunities? Everyone is familiar with the largest companies in a geographic area, and every vendor has Sisyphus-like sales representatives calling on them. They may have never asked themselves the most basic questions: Are they pushing the right rock or product? Have they selected the right hill or customer? Could their time and effort be better rewarded elsewhere?

The job of prospecting is actually easier than it used to be. We no longer need to cold call or go "smoke stacking" hoping to find a thriving business in need of our products and services. You can sip your morning coffee in your pajamas, log in, and learn just about anything you want to know about a company within your target market or industry.

So the challenge is to pursue business opportunities with the highest likelihood of success. Your products may fit many markets: hospitals, clinics, and medical supply houses; food processors; packaging equipment makers; paper mills; retail merchandisers; oil refineries; and so on. Unless you are a specialist in a given industry, you may find yourself challenged even as a sales veteran to prospect in a market segment less familiar to you. Professional associations can be a big help. TAPPI, in the pulp and paper industry, has complete process training materials available at a nominal charge, as does SEMI, the Society of Automotive Engineers, and the IEEE, to name just a few. Take a tour. Breweries, food plants, paper mills, electronics companies, automobile and motorcycle plants, and many more offer public tours. Go to the company's website, or call the main office to find out when and where. On the tour, ask questions, and notice the machinery, the brands, the names for the stages in the process, the pace. Watch the movie, pick up the literature, and sample the products if offered. Listen for terms that are unfamiliar to you, or for terms that are pronounced differently in this industry than they would be in general. For example, you may think the word *couch* represents something to sit on, but if you're in a paper mill, you had better know what it does and that it's pronounced *kooch*.

For each of your prospects, you develop a plan. Using a mix of "touches," you plan how best to use your time. For example, you may establish your call plan for your top ten prospects as follows:

Company	Title	1	2	3	4	5	6
MegaCorp	VP Engin.	Call	E-mail	Call	Note	Call	Event
SuprSteel	VP Engin.	Call	E-mail	Call	Note	Call	Event

The frequency here might be every week or every other week, or, as one of the best "hunters" I know does it, you may begin by calling at different times without leaving a message until you actually get the prospect on the phone. The hunter then states his twenty-second message consisting of his name, business experience, and a request for a brief meeting. After that initial contact, he may get a longer phone conversation or a first appointment, or he may commit to sending out some information. Only then does he plan his follow-up campaign.

In addition to calls, e-mails, and notes, you may use newsletters. Don't sign a prospect up without her permission but send a sample with a note and, in your follow-up, ask if the prospect is interested in receiving it or whether there might be someone else in their organization who would appreciate it. High-level managers usually appreciate news about the industry and other companies, while techno-types and project engineers might be more appreciative of software and product news.

If your company offers seminars, classes, or other customer events, make sure you get your customers onto the mailing list and be careful to identify them by the appropriate level. Special events like open houses or trade shows may have invitations you can hand-carry; but they are potential supplemental mailings as well, especially if you alert your customer with a phone call ahead of time that an invitation is on its way.

Prior to a first meeting, send a brief e-mail confirming the details of time and place and listing some of the questions you will want to discuss. After the meeting, a note confirming what you learned avoids confusion and keeps you from charging along based on what you think you heard. It also allows the customer to clue you in immediately if you were making assumptions that proved faulty, sparing embarrassment later. Including a brochure before a meeting is unwise because it directs the conversation toward product prematurely when the salesperson with soul should be focused on the business issues and goals of the customer. It also allows the customer to form his own conclusions, right or wrong, and you may not get an opportunity to clarify or to learn more. Sending a brochure after the meeting may be helpful, but take the time to circle and mark it up to show that you were listening and to reinforce the points you feel are the most beneficial. Remember, most brochures are intended for general consumption and may include information that actually turns off your customer or raises concerns in his mind.

Sending out a video link, a clip from a newspaper or magazine, or other material that would be of interest to your key contacts is a good idea. Keep your eyes open for material of interest that can be used to keep you in front of your prospects.

There are also services available to help you prospect for new business. Constant Contact and others manage e-mail lists and updates; services like Articles to Go provide newsletters you can send out over your own company name; and a variety of other companies provide lead generation and follow-up services

Whenever you communicate electronically with your prospects and customers, remember a few basic rules of netiquette, as explained below by my imaginary friend, Miss E. Milly Post:

1. Don't send me e-mails I'll have to scroll up and down my screen to read. If I have to scroll up and down, it means it's too gosh-darned long, and it will be much easier to just delete it than to keep it cluttering up my inbox until I have a printer available.
2. Don't send me e-mails with graphics that will take half a day to download when you can just send me a link.
3. Don't even think about sending me anything electronically that I'd be embarrassed to have lying on my desk in hard copy.
4. Don't put anything in e-mail you wouldn't want to appear as part of a legal deposition.
5. Don't put anything in e-mail that you wouldn't want to hear Mike Wallace read on *60 Minutes*.
6. Don't put it in e-mail just because you're too darned lazy to write a good old-fashioned thank you note or letter of congratulations or, God forbid, a note of condolence. In my opinion, the only proper way to express these sentiments is in your own hand on your own note card.
7. Sending me a text is okay only if you have my permission to do so. Otherwise, you are interrupting me and intruding on my time. Please don't assume I will welcome your text.

Well, I sincerely hope these guidelines will help you to be a better e-citizen and to preserve the manners that are at the very heart of our civilization.

REFLECTIONS ON CHAPTER 7
Getting the First Appointment

You have to recognize when the right place and the right time fuse and take advantage of that opportunity. There are plenty of opportunities out there. You can't sit back and wait.
—Ellen Metcalf

Self-knowledge is essential to self-improvement. Take some time to reflect on what may be keeping you from reaching out to people who can benefit from the products and services you provide.

1. What's keeping you from picking up that telephone and calling a prospective new customer? Fear of rejection? Fear of the stereotype of salespeople? Are you afraid he'll be rude? Yell at you? Call you names? Has that ever actually happened?
Put that stereotype aside and ask yourself these questions:
Do I take good care of my customers?
Have I helped them solve their business problems?
Am I honest and ethical in my business dealings?
Are there people who would benefit from what I offer?
How can I help them?
2. Are you prepared to prospect? Have you put together a list of companies you would like to do business with? Have you researched them on the Internet and learned the names of the people who would most benefit from what you offer?
3. Have you identified the business issues that are likely to concern that person? Are you prepared to give an example of how you or your company has been able to help other customers address those concerns?
4. Remind yourself that it is easier to start at the top and be delegated down to a technical evaluator or a user than it is to start at the bottom and try to work your way up. Starting at the user level and hoping you have found someone with enough influence to get you to the right level may be easier, but what are the odds for success?
5. Do you have a plan for how you will reach your prospects? Have you created a call/mail/call sequence of reaching out

with business issues? Have you found a success story or a white paper that might be interesting to your customers? How many times will you try to reach out before giving up for now?

6. If you try five times to find a contact within a company who is willing to talk with you and you fail, when will you try again? If this prospect is really strategic for you, don't let three months pass by without some attempt at making a successful contact.

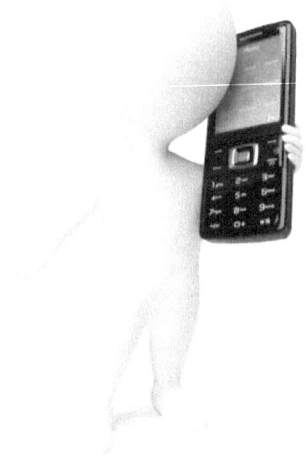

Remember: There are people out there who need what you sell.

CHAPTER 8

Qualifying: Respecting Yourself And Your Customer

You got the appointment. You asked for a brief meeting, and she agreed. Now you must keep your word by being brief, prepared, and focused on the customer and the problem she wants to solve. Remember, she didn't agree to meet with you because she is lonely. She is hopeful that you can help her. So ask your questions, but do so with empathy for the customer. Treat him with respect, both by the nature and type of your questions and by the length of time you take to ask them. If you scheduled your appointment for thirty minutes, don't take an hour. Many salespeople ask, "But what if they're doing all the talking? Shouldn't I let them talk as long as they want to?"

What message do you send if you stay long after your meeting was scheduled to end? You're saying you didn't mean it when you asked for half an hour. You're saying you have no other appointments you have to get to. You're saying once your foot is in the door, the customer is going to have to kick you out. Selling with soul requires respecting both yourself and your customer.

When your half hour is up, say, "I've taken all the time you agreed to give me. I still have some questions. Shall we schedule another appointment?" If the customer says, "No, let's just talk more now," you need to set a limit. For example, you may say, "Great. I have twenty minutes before I need to leave for my next meeting. Let's continue."

If you have done a good job of planning your day and your time, you will most certainly have another appointment. If you have not, then consider the "next meeting" you referred to as an appointment with yourself. Leave. Get a cup of coffee. And make phone calls to fill your day planner with appointments, research, or follow-up. Remember, time spent preparing well is essential to selling with soul. "Winging it" shows disrespect for your customer and for your own most valuable resource, your time.

Before you leave, ask for the opportunity to come back and review with him or her what you've learned and how your product may be used to help. Ask for the names of people in the organization whom he or she respects and relies on for input before making a decision. Schedule your follow-up appointments, both with this customer and with the people he refers you to if possible.

Veteran salespeople know that first you must sell yourself, then your company, and only after that, your product. Selling yourself requires that you demonstrate professionalism, integrity, and respect for your customer. When we have Bob's balance, our priorities are clear. We enjoy what author Spencer Johnson in *The One Minute $ales Person* calls "The Wonderful Paradox": "I have more fun and enjoy more financial success when I stop trying to get what I want and start helping other people get what they want."

What Should You Accomplish in the First Appointment?
Selling Yourself

Integrity is defined in a Webster dictionary as "honesty, soundness, unimpaired condition." By now you have demonstrated your honesty by stating you'll call at a specific time to request this appointment and then doing so. You will now demonstrate "soundness" by your level of preparation and logical reasoning. We'll assume you've arrived properly dressed and in "unimpaired condition." This is the stage of selling that Neil Rackham, author of *SPIN Selling*, calls the "preliminaries," and he offers research to show that it is not as important as salespeople are traditionally taught it is. The first order of business is to let the customer know, briefly, who you are and why he or she was wise to agree to see you. You are expected to introduce yourself and your company briefly, even if you have covered this information in your previous notes and letters.

The helpful exercise that follows was actually developed to help salespeople with "on the spot" situations. It can also help you prepare to do an effective and efficient job in the preliminaries stage of a sales call.

Imagine you find yourself in an elevator with the president of the company, someone you have wanted to meet for months. You have been told repeatedly, "The president doesn't see sales reps." You have the time it takes to travel four floors to impress him enough that he will make an exception. What will you say? Do you have a tagline that sets you apart? When companies are building their brands, they use brief taglines to convey a quality they want associated with what they sell. For example, "Don't Leave Home Without It," "I'm Lovin' It," and "Just Do It" immediately bring the names American Express, McDonalds, and Nike to mind. What would you want yours to be? Is it, "I help manufacturers achieve their quality goals"? Or are you focused on solving people problems, helping customers save money, helping them improve a process?

When asked to introduce ourselves at a meeting or a social gathering, many of us go brain-dead. We can barely remember our name, let alone think of something of importance to say about ourselves. We are afraid of sounding egotistical or stupid or both. Preparing your introduction, and practicing it so you are ready to do it quickly and with confidence, sets you apart.

The chances are good that the other person will not remember your name from hearing it once. By associating your name with a credential, you increase the probability of being remembered. For example:

"Mr. Executive, I'm Sharon Parker with XYZ Company. I've been working closely with Joe Smith in Information Systems to find ways to make your manufacturing reports more timely."

"Oh, how do you do?"

"I'm curious. Is there other information you wish you could get? Or a report that would be more helpful to you if it were more timely? Or shorter?"

Don't expect a detailed answer at this point. After all, you've probably reached his floor. But regardless of what he says, do extend your hand and restate your name, adding how happy you are to have met him and that you appreciate the opportunity to work with his staff. Of course, if he asks you to join him in his office so he can give you a better answer to your question, don't hesitate. Just keep this impromptu session very brief out of respect for his time—and don't try to get all your questions answered today. Ask if you can make a short return visit instead.

In your first sales call at a company, you will not be limited to elevator time, but you may still find yourself sitting in the lobby or a vendor area rather than being invited into your prospect's office. You are on probation here. Make your introduction short and clear, and get to the point. State your name, your company, and why you requested the meeting. As you hand the customer your business card, simply state:

"I'm glad we could meet. I've been with XYZ Company three years and have worked with a number of paper (or packaging or pharmaceutical—be specific!) firms in your industry. We've been able to help our customers improve efficiency (or save money, improve quality, etc., based on your earlier homework), and I'm hoping you and I can find a way to do the same thing together here."

Be prepared, of course, to name several companies with whom your employer has earned a solid reference in case you are immediately asked to back up that statement.

Now it's time to demonstrate that your interest is in him and his problems.

"Would you tell me a little bit about yourself? How long have you been with the company? What are your main goals at this time?"

Take out your notebook, unless you have a photographic memory, and start writing. If you see any sign of discomfort from your customer, ask his or her permission to take notes for yourself as a memory aid. You'll want these notes later when you send your follow-up letter or e-mail summarizing this meeting and asking the customer for the next one.

Five Ws and an H

Reporters are told to answer certain questions as early as possible in every story. These questions are often referred to as the five *W*s and the *H*: Who? What? Where? When? Why? How? Salespeople must have these answers as well, in order to determine if they can help the customer. Let's look at each of them in turn.

Who involves a number of questions for the customer. Who are you? What is your area of responsibility? Who do you report to? Who will you involve in evaluating my products and services? These are simple and straightforward questions. Each one, however, has the potential to either demonstrate your empathy or exhibit only self-interest.

For example, "Who do you report to?" sounds logical. But put yourself in the customer's position; in other words, use your empathy or ability to "emotionally or intellectually identify with another." If someone you barely know asked you who you report to, would your defenses kick in? Would you wonder if she were immediately planning to "go over your head"? Would you worry she might use your name to get in to see your boss? I would. Most of us would. Remember, we are all adults physically, but we carry inside us insecurities and emotions from our entire history. It is a rare corporation or business that makes its employees feel secure in their positions and respected for their abilities to the extent that they are free of defensive responses.

A better way to approach this might be to ask your customer how the company is organized functionally and where his department fits into the overall organization. He may even give you an organization chart.

How about the question "Who will make this decision?" Most of us were taught to find the decision maker immediately, so we throw that question into the fray in the first call in case our sales manager asks us for it when we get back. Invoke your empathy once again and see yourself responding to the question "Who will make this decision?"

Ouch. Feel a little slighted? Underestimated? Whether or not the customer is the only person in her entire company who will be involved in making this decision, the tendency of most customers is to immediately respond, "I will," whether it's true or not.

Why? First of all, they are not about to let you treat them with disrespect, and they know many salespeople who will do just that if they suspect someone else is the decision maker. Second, they want to control your activity in this account and make certain you are not going to other people, using their name for entry and bringing down on their heads the wrath of managers who blame them for giving another attack-dog salesperson their scent.

Wouldn't it make a lot more sense to assume they will make the decision and, instead, ask them who they rely on for input before doing so? Wouldn't you rather be asked who you might involve in the decision-making process?

If you stand in the customer's shoes for a moment, it's easy to see why so many salespeople are written off as rude and self-serving in the first few minutes of a call.

Keep the who discussion brief and remember that, as a problem solver, your main concern is *what*. Remember, our value proposition is that you are going to do something for them and they are going to do something for you. Understanding the customer's goal or business issue is essential to aligning with his needs rather than trying to force a solution you just happen to sell. Remember that he may say things like, "We want to upgrade our line, modernize, and so on." That's not a goal. That's a means to achieve a goal, perhaps, and there may be many other ways to achieve it as well. When you hear phrases that describe "goals" but they can't be quantified in terms of value or financial benefit, they're not goals. The wise seller will question further. "Why do you want to modernize? What do you expect from that effort?"

Some of the key questions here are:

What is the most critical part of your operation? What is your biggest business challenge? Or, put another way, what problem are you trying to solve? What goal are you trying to achieve?

How do you address this issue today? What works well? What do you wish worked differently? What would you change if you could?

You need to understand *where* and *when* your solution might first be tried. How does this customer implement a change? Is there a department or an area that might be used as a pilot? Is there another group that has to be involved in any new implementation, perhaps central engineering, corporate headquarters, information systems? You need to understand the fiscal year of this customer, including when they do budget planning, when they have shutdowns or slow periods in their business cycle, and when they might be willing to make changes to the process you're discussing. You also need to know when you might be able to talk with other people in the company to complete your information gathering, and whether or not this customer will help you do so. And you also need to know when the company normally makes a decision on projects such as yours and how much time might be involved in the evaluation period.

The last W, *why*, is a tricky one. Asking someone why he did something often triggers a defensive reaction. We want to focus on the future, not the past. Instead of asking why she wants to achieve a particular goal, we might ask what will be better when she does achieve it. Instead of asking why this particular problem is his focus, we might ask what the benefit will be of solving it.

Finally, you need to understand the buying process this customer follows by asking the customer *how* you can gather the information you need to determine whether or not you have a solution to his or her problem. Will he help you schedule an appointment with another person at the company who handles a tangential area? Will she allow you to meet with one of her users or operators or direct reports to get his or her perspective? Will he provide you with sample reports or copies of the current operation for your reference?

How will she make the decision? How many people will be involved? How many alternatives might they consider? Do they have to solicit three proposals, or are they free to work with you exclusively? Will they prepare a request for proposals? Will you be doing a demonstration of your final recommendation? How does the buying process work at this customer's business, and what is required of you and him to facilitate an evaluation? How does this customer measure value? Do they use a hurdle rate, payback time estimate, return on investment, company-developed analysis tool?

While you cannot know all the factors the customer takes into account, such as their internal cost of capital or what other internal projects are competing with this one for time and money, you can focus your value statements on what the customer has actually told you. When he trusts that you are aligned with them and focused on their goals, he will provide you with cost information like how much an hour of manufacturing downtime costs, how much they spend to hire and train a new employee, how much turnover of valued employees costs them, and other details that you can use to compare the cost of this project to the cost of the problem it addresses and the value the customer expects to receive. While all the details may not be known or shared in the first call, you want to gather as much information as you can to help you put your own project timeline together.

When you ask these same questions of other people in the company, you may get different answers. Each and every one of us has our own perspective on what's important or what the best way is to get something done. Selling with soul requires us to be amateur psychologists in many ways and to understand our own opinions, biases, and emotions as well as to understand those of our customers. It helps to ask key questions three times in three different ways. Why? Counselors are trained to get three answers to any important question as a way of getting at underlying motives and intentions. Salespeople can benefit from this same principle. The first answers will reflect a contact's rational and intellectual view of the situation. Often the second will add data or information to support that response. On a third response, however, many people will reveal an emotional component to the answer that helps you understand their true intention or desire.

The higher the price of your solution or the more complex it is to implement, the greater the probability that you will be selling to a committee or a task force, rather than to one individual. This is the corporate "spread-the-risk" philosophy, also expressed as "if you might go down in flames, make sure you don't go down alone." This lengthens the sales cycle and makes it vital that you stay current on your information, that you verify everything you've been told, and that you remain honest and centered in your integrity and your soul throughout.

Many salespeople make the mistake of trying to be all things to all people. They change their look and their style with every customer, hoping to increase their acceptability. Some sales trainers emphasize "versatility" as the most important selling trait, urging you to size up your customer as an analytical detail type, a bottom-line or cut-to-the-chase type, a good buddy social type, or a people-pleaser peacemaking type. As discussed in Chapter 4, "The Matter of Personal Styles," there are different ways to "type" a customer's personality. Some sales managers recommend that you adjust your personality to fit that box.

However, few things broadcast dishonesty as loudly and as far as trying to be someone you're not. If you are adjusting your style to fit someone else, you are going to be and appear to be as uncomfortable as if you were wearing someone else's suit. Your own soul will chafe and itch throughout the experience. Empathy is vital; adaptation is not. If you understand your customer to be a social, storytelling person whose office is filled with photos, plaques, and trophies, be prepared to listen and laugh appreciatively. Do *not* try to go in with a story or joke of your own unless you are also an expressive type and the two of you have an area of interest in common. Rather, put yourself in his shoes and realize that applause and appreciation are important to this person. Any solution you propose should offer that as one of its benefits. Then, make sure that your presentation to this customer shows how your solution will benefit *his* customers, whether internal or external. By so doing, you satisfy his "type" needs and do so with respect. You do not, however, compromise your own style and your own integrity in the process.

Similarly, if your customer is analytical and wants to see all the details, if her office overflows with computer printouts and spreadsheets, you will make sure your presentation, and your solution, provide a level of detail that can satisfy her that it is thorough and well thought-out. If you are a big-picture or concept kind of person, you may prefer to skip this part of the proposal. Salespeople who are impatient with details themselves often lapse into the "trust me" stance when confronted with someone who requires the analysis to be confident in recommending your solution.

Put yourself in her place and ask yourself if you would submit to major surgery without the doctor explaining to you and your family what exactly would be done, what the risks were, and what the recovery period would involve. No one is going to "put me under" unless I know the plan—in detail. And for many of our customers, a new product or service is the equivalent of performing major surgery on their business. There is a lengthy period of recovery after the operation is performed. Aren't they entitled to the details?

As we go through the qualifying process, it helps to remember the old adage "never assume." Breaking the word *assume* into its letters, the saying continues: "When you assume, you make an 'ass' out of 'u' and 'me.'" Ask the same questions of several people. Get their differing points of view. Compare the answers you get to help you identify potential areas for misunderstanding or concerns about your product or service. By now, you are forming some preliminary ideas in your head as to how your product or service can help this customer solve his problem. Test some of them in your follow-up calls. Get as much feedback as possible. There's no need to hedge. Your customers know you are a salesperson. Be proud of that fact and enthusiastic in seeking ideas and feedback to help you shape your solution.

It's important, also, to keep confirming the information you get as you make follow-up calls. Some of what you hear will directly conflict with information you have. Dissimilar versions of the truth may leave you wondering if your customer is lying. While we all meet dishonest people in the course of our daily lives, a more likely explanation is that each person you meet sees only part of the picture. Many corporations, believing knowledge is power, keep the big picture from their employees, doling out bits of information as begrudgingly as a taskmaster allocating gruel in a Dickensian orphanage. Because each person must base his conclusions on the pieces of information he has and cannot take into account the pieces that are hidden from him, the answers to your questions may remind you of the parable of the blind men describing the elephant. The one feeling the trunk thinks he has a snakelike creature, while the one feeling the leg thinks it may be a large tree.

Selling with soul means that we approach the critical step of qualifying an opportunity with thorough preparation, respect for ourselves and our customer, an attitude of empathy, and a sincere desire to help the customer achieve her goal. With that approach we will learn what we need to learn in order to invest additional resources in an opportunity—or admit to ourselves that this one is not a fit for us and move on. It is better to admit to ourselves and our customer early that we do not have the right solution and preserve the trust we built to get the appointments in the first place than to waste time and resources, both our own and our customers, on a problem we cannot help solve.

REFLECTIONS ON CHAPTER 8
Qualifying: Respecting Yourself and Your Customer

Time is the coin of your life. It is the only coin you have, and only you can determine how it will be spent. Be careful lest you let other people spend it for you.
—Carl Sandburg

Time and knowledge are precious assets. By preparing thoroughly and confirming often, you make the best use of your time and show respect for yourself and your customer. Ask yourself the questions below.

1. If you were to write a tagline for yourself as a salesperson, what would you want it to be? What skills are you most proud of? What do you want people to say about your professional behavior?

2. Write your elevator speech and include your name, your company, and your tagline, as well as a relevant question for the person you meet. Practice it so that it is the first thing that comes to mind when you introduce yourself to others.

3. Do you take the time to prepare your questions before a call? While it is vital that you listen to a customer's answer and follow his concerns, how do you make sure you learn enough to evaluate this opportunity? If you wing it, do you often think of things you wish you had asked when you had the first opportunity?

4. Do you confirm what you heard in a first meeting by sending a brief note or summary outlining it? If not, how do you know you truly understood what the customer said?

5. Are you honest in your evaluation of whether or not this is a good fit for your product and services? Trying to bend the facts or basing your efforts on a future product enhancement rather than on what you can actually deliver prevents you and

your customer from putting your time and resources to the best use today.

Figure 5. I respect both my own and my customer's time.

CHAPTER 9

Presenting Your Solution

HAVING DONE A THOROUGH job of researching and understanding the problem facing your customer, you have now earned the right to present your solution. This, for salespeople who thrive on recognition and crave an audience is the moment of glory. For other salespeople, making a presentation is terrifying and could only be made worse by having to do it naked or being required to sing it. All eyes will be on you; and, even though you've done a lot to demonstrate your value proposition as a problem solver, the very act of presenting or "pitching" is sure to raise the customer's level of cynicism. Everything you say and do will be questioned by people who have come to believe that a sales pitch is as genuine as professional wrestling and as entertaining as a root canal. How do you handle this pivotal point in the sales cycle with soul? Remember our watchwords: integrity and empathy.

If you have empathy for your customer, you will not present features or benefits that are irrelevant to them just because they are part of the standard "pitch" sent you by your marketing department. If you have empathy, you will not give examples from other industries or businesses with no resemblance to their own. If you have empathy, you will not exceed your allotted time, and you will have allowed in your preplanning for a question period. And, finally, if you have empathy, you will have practiced. And practiced some more. And practiced yet again. But more on that later.

Begin your presentation with a brief summary of what you have learned about the problem and how to go about solving it. Preparing this in bullet format brings everyone in the room to the same focus and reestablishes you as being aligned around their needs. It shows you have done the homework and banishes the specter of any former self-interested salespeople from the room.

Once you have reviewed the elements of the problem, review how the capabilities of your product or service can be used by them to solve their problem or achieve their goal. Do not list features or capabilities that are irrelevant to your customer. If you can't answer the question "Why should they care about this?" leave it out.

Now, you have set the stage and told them what you're going to tell them. Dale Carnegie would be proud of you. Ask for a verification that the agenda you just laid out meets their expectations. If it doesn't, you still have time for a correction in emphasis or content. If it does, you're ready to go.

In your presentation, you will highlight the features or capabilities of your product that will play a part in the customer solving his problem. You will help them develop a vision of themselves and their team using these capabilities to achieve the results they are looking for. You will not exaggerate or misrepresent your product's capabilities nor will you sell "futures." If your product is not yet capable of accomplishing a task the customer requires but you know the next release will provide that capability, you will say so, and you will be as accurate as you can about the date of the next release. Many companies have a long history of "slipping" in their release dates, and if yours is one of them, make certain you set your customer's expectations accordingly. It does no good to paint yourself as a hero now, only to blame "the factory" or "marketing" or "product engineering" later, when you are unable to deliver on your promise. Remember, to your customer you *are* the factory and marketing and product engineering. You cannot differentiate yourself from the company whose name appears on your paycheck. Pointing a finger, as every kindergartner knows, leaves four fingers pointing right back at you.

Selling future capabilities is a very risky approach. When as salespeople we were told a particular product would have a vital capability in the next release, we were skeptical based on our past experience. If we were told it would be out in April, we would ask "April of what year?" Don't fall into the futures trap and leave your customer feeling misled. You will be selling more soulfully by acknowledging that a capability is planned but that you cannot be certain of when it will be deliverable. If you have a work-around (another way to solve the problem for now that may not be optimal), go ahead and present it. After all, what you are selling here is really a long-term business relationship, not a one-shot deal, and you want your customer to know that you will still be here to work with her on implementing a better solution as soon as it becomes available

Remember to keep your presentation focused on the customer's problem and your solution to it. Do not waste his time with features that are irrelevant to the problem at hand, even if you think they are the neatest things since sliced bread. And do not go over your allotted time. Too many excellent presentations fizzle into failure as the customers begin checking their watches and the sales rep talks faster and faster, starting sentences with "and one last thing."

There's an old story about a preacher who was dismayed to see only one parishioner in the church on a sunny Sunday morning. He asked the parishioner what he should do, and the man replied, "Well, if I went out to feed the sheep and only one showed up, I reckon I'd feed him." So the preacher went on to deliver his full sermon, working himself up into quite an emotional state in the process. After about twenty minutes, he looked up and saw the man walking out. "Hey! Where are you going?" he called out. "I thought you said I should feed the sheep, even if there was only one." The parishioner turned around and replied, "Yeah, but I sure wouldn't feed him the whole wagonload." You, too, should remember to feed the sheep, not bury them.

Whether you've been selling for twenty years or two months, the key to a successful presentation is practice. Only by practicing, out loud, can you test your own knowledge. Only by practicing, out loud, can you accurately time your presentation to make sure you will not run overtime. And only by practicing, out loud, will you find the difficult-to-pronounce words and awkward phrases that can trip you up and cause embarrassment at the worst possible time. I once heard a sales engineer speak on programming techniques. He repeatedly mispronounced "sequential function chart" in a way that would have earned him an "R" rating in Hollywood.

Is there anything more annoying than watching a presenter fumble with cords and switches and focus, and finally ask, "Is there anybody here who knows how to run this thing?" Whether you use an antique overhead projector or the latest in video technology, know your equipment and bring your own. Being dependent on the customer's technology puts you at the mercy of what's available at that moment and on whether or not someone in your audience knows how to use it, troubleshoot it, or find a "spare" if needed. Know how to set up your equipment and focus it. Test the view from several places in the room. And for heaven's sake, bring your own extension cord, spare projector bulb, or backup disk. One note of caution: Even after you've done a thousand customer presentations, you can be caught by surprise. I recently switched from a PC to a MacBook and am grateful that my clients were patient with me while I figured out the differences and tried to modify my materials for the different technology. Had they been prospects, I would not have been so fortunate.

Practice shows respect for your audience, and that is an important element in selling with soul. Once you have practiced to a level of confidence and clarity, practice once more. It is also a good idea to have someone from your team take notes and observe the reactions of your audience. He or she can make note of any remaining questions as well as list any follow-up items the customer may request.

And in conclusion …

No matter how thorough your presentation, a weak ending will leave you and your customer flat. Don't fall back on "Does anybody have any questions?" A better way to conclude is with some questions of your own, such as, "Does this approach make sense to you? Will it solve the problem? Are there areas that are not clear or that you would like me to go over in more detail?"

If everyone agrees that your presentation showed a realistic and practical solution to the problem at hand, you have earned the right to ask for the order. This will often reveal objections that did not surface earlier. How do you respond? More on that follows.

REFLECTIONS ON CHAPTER 9
Presenting Your Solution

People don't want to buy a quarter-inch drill. They want a quarter-inch hole!
—Dr. Theodore Levitt

Have you ever made the mistake of blaming your audience for not getting your message? Presenting effectively is not a one-way process but an interactive one. It is by asking questions, clarifying and confirming as we present, that we engage our audience and communicate effectively.

1. Have you sent an agenda confirming that you and the customer have the same expectations for your meeting?

2. Have you verified who will be in attendance and asked each one what his or her objective is for the meeting?

3. Have you practiced your presentation out loud so your brain has a chance to hear your mouth say it right? This alone can significantly reduce the possibility of making misstatements or errors in the tension of the actual moment.

4. Have you tested all your equipment so you are confident with it and verified whether any other equipment you may need (flip charts, whiteboard) will be in the room?

5. Will you or someone from your team take careful notes during the presentation and observe body language so you can make sure any concerns are discussed?

6. Have you already marked your calendar to send follow-up e-mails or letters following the presentation summarizing the main points covered?

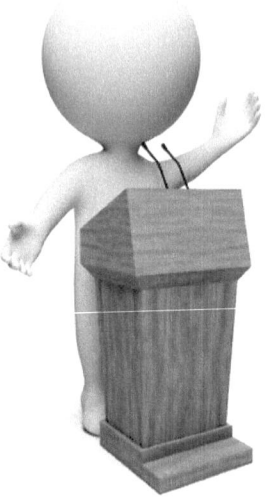

Figure 6. The customer determines what we present by telling us what she needs to solve her problem.

CHAPTER 10

Discovering And Responding To Concerns

How many ways does a customer have to say "no"? Every concern raised is a no unless you have taken the time to understand what is behind it, test alternative ideas, and align with the customer to create a shared vision of the solution. Because we have proceeded throughout the sales process with an expectation of mutual benefit, we approach these final stages the same way. What is the customer going to do for us? What are we going to do for the customer? Never is this more clear than when you are discussing price.

When a customer says your product is too expensive, most salespeople hear this as the start of haggling over price, and all too many immediately offer a discount. In fact, many salespeople offer a discount or set the expectation of one without the customer even asking for it. For example, answering the question about what it costs by citing the list price and then quickly adding, "but we can always find ways to discount that," tells the customer you do not think your product is worth the list price to begin with. If you have worked with the customer to identify the value of your solution, you have earned the right to sell your product and service at a level that is profitable for your own company at the same time that it helps the customer solve his or her problem. Let's look at "expensive" another way.

The customer may be telling you he is not convinced that the value he will receive equals or exceeds the price being quoted. You have not shown your customer enough benefit, and as a result, he cannot proceed with confidence that his investment will net a worthwhile return. Don't forget: In most cases, your buyer will have to justify his decision to another level of management and may even be asked to defend it to people with different goals or a different preferred approach. You need to help your customer see the value and quantify it.

How do you quantify value? Accountants will tell you there are hard and soft costs associated with any investment, and purchasing your product should be viewed as exactly that: an investment. Some of the hard costs that may be involved include purchase price, warranty extension, installation, wiring and cabling, supplies, spares or replacement parts, training employees to use the product, and maintenance.

Soft costs include the time people spend evaluating the product and planning for its implementation, disruption of schedules, time spent in training, delays in completing normal tasks due to learning new procedures, reduced productivity, and employee frustration or reduced morale as people adjust to the change. Quantifying these may not ever be discussed, but in your customer's mind, they are part of the price she is going to pay for your proposed solution. That makes it critical that you be able to demonstrate and quantify as accurately as possible the benefits that will be received.

Like costs, benefits come in both the hard and the soft variety. Hard benefits include cost savings or cost displacement, faster throughput, reduced maintenance fees, reduced downtime, and elimination of manual or people-intensive steps in a process. Soft benefits include improved quality, increased flexibility or a wider range of options to offer your internal or external customers, enhanced skills for your employees, and being able to differentiate yourself from your competitors.

All these benefits can be quantified; however, you and your customer must agree on the measuring device. Discussing all of the benefits beforehand and agreeing on a fair metric to assign them, whether it is dollars, hours, percentages, number of occurrences, or another value, is an important part of the qualifying step in the sales cycle. If you fail to do this thoroughly, you will pay the price when objections are raised to your proposed solution.

What if the customer objects that your solution is more expensive than a competitor's? Do you ask how much more and prepare to "drop your shorts" on pricing? Many salespeople do, only to learn later that the competition is offering a less complete solution or is lowballing their proposal, which in business selling is the equivalent of bait and switch in retail. You can help the customer compare the two solutions benefit for benefit if you choose to, but it is never a good idea to focus the discussion on the competition. Your value proposition is based on what you are going to do for the customer, not what someone else may or may not provide.

Never fall into the trap of bad-mouthing your competitor. None of us, no matter how much we might enjoy a juicy bit of gossip, respects people who bad-mouth others. There is always a residual feeling that if they're passing on dirt about that guy, they are just as likely to pass on dirt about me in the future. Integrity requires that you be honest and true to your own value. The customer will respect the difference. It is your job to know the strengths and weaknesses of your competitors. It is also your responsibility to know what differentiates your product from theirs. Focus on your strengths, not their weaknesses.

A more meaningful response to a customer who uses the competition to challenge you is to show him the value he can expect to receive for dollar invested. And don't forget to include the soft benefits as you step him back through the discussion of how he sees your product and service solving his problem. For example, say, "I can't speak to my competitor's proposal, but I do know that you and your team have told me the capabilities we're proposing will allow them to solve the problem and achieve good value. Is that still true?" Remind the customer of the work you have done together and the reasons you have come to this point in the first place.

If, in fact, you respond by dropping your price with either of these first two objections, you have just told the customer you were asking more for it than you should have in the first place. And where does that leave your integrity? Customers don't buy from people they like; they buy from people they respect.

Going back to our basic value proposition, if you are doing something for her in the way of reducing the price, what is the customer going to do for you? Mutual benefit demands that there be an exchange. Will the customer purchase an additional training class? Will she agree to purchase additional volume based on the satisfactory performance of your first installation? Will she standardize on your product? If she insists cost is the only issue, what is she willing to give up? Has the project plan grown to a point she doesn't really need? Has she thought about what it will cost her to delay implementation or to leave the problem unsolved? What will it cost her to start over with a new evaluation?

Remember that your proposal is based on providing the customer good value, and if he wants to reduce the price, there has to be some additional benefit to your company in exchange. Just giving up margin reinforces the negative attitudes toward salespeople. Customers are people first. They don't necessarily need to feel they are getting the lowest price. They *do* need to feel they are getting good value for their investment. When a seller gives a discount before the customer even asks for one, the seller is just setting the expectation that there is more money there to be given away.

Some sellers routinely inflate the price they quote so that they have dollars they can discount at negotiation time. There are problems with this approach if your goal is to sell with soul. First, of course, you are not being honest about the actual price, so what does that say about your integrity? Second, you are training your customer to squeeze you on price because there is always something extra to be gained. Is this how you want to negotiate? Selling with soul requires that we work together with our customer along the way to the purchase to fully understand the problem, help her see what a successful implementation will require, and help her develop a vision of what it will look like when her people solve the problem using your products and services. Wouldn't you rather be able to say when squeezed, "Knowing you want to receive the most value for this investment, I have worked hard with your people over the past months to drive out any unnecessary costs. This is the price."

Some salespeople are so afraid of saying "no" to a customer that they agree to any and all requests, no matter how unreasonable, throughout the selling process in hope of just getting to the final negotiation. By doing so, they have given all of their personal and professional power away and have trained the customer that they will say yes reflexively to avoid losing. It is important to say no and to mean it when appropriate. Ask yourself how many times you have agreed to do things for a customer that should have been his or her responsibility. Have you given away things that you could have and should have charged for? Have you had to beg forgiveness from your sales manager for accepting an unreasonable time frame or demand?

Until you say no, the customer has every reason to believe you have more to give away. Practice stating with confidence, "We've worked hard together to put together a proposal that accurately meets your requirements and adds value. The price is final."

There are excellent training programs on effective negotiating, and all include the importance of being comfortable saying no at appropriate times. They also teach "quid pro quo," or getting something before you give something. *CustomerCentric Selling*®, for example, offers training in this and all the other key elements of the buying cycle. Codeveloped by Mike Bosworth, who formerly developed *Solution Selling*, it is the best example I've seen of helping salespeople build on a proven process and improve their results at each step.

Not all objections are about price. When a customer objects to a feature of your product, its footprint or size, its cosmetic appearance, or its expected life cycle, he is expressing concerns that may seem trivial to you. Some salespeople take it personally. Selling with soul requires that we use our empathy to find out *why* these are issues. "Too big" may actually be about where your product can be placed or installed. If the plan is to put it in the accounting department but it won't physically fit in the room, there are cabling and installation issues to be addressed. And if it's not going to be physically near the people who will use it and troubleshoot it, there are productivity and span of control issues as well. If you're talking with an original equipment manufacturer (OEM) who is considering incorporating your product into a machine or product he resells, footprint can be a crucial element in the overall cost of his finished product, as well as a concern for his end customers. Only when you take the time to find out and understand the underlying issues can you determine whether you have a way to address them.

Cosmetic concerns, like color or the shape of buttons or other details, may also indicate more than personal preference. Perhaps she is looking for a very visible difference to emphasize the new approach. Unless you ask the customer what she would change and how she would change it to make it perfect, you may not learn how deep this objection runs. Asking, as well, how much more she might be willing to pay to have that change made will help you to prioritize her wish list. The better you understand, the better you can address the concern.

Finally, remember that it is easier for a customer to reject your product than it is for him to reject you, especially after you have spent a lot of time together working on a proposed solution. A product objection may be a nonpersonal way to tell you that you won't get the sale. Only by asking good questions can you determine the truth.

Our customers face the same challenges we do. They are often given an assignment with an unreasonable deadline, or are asked to get something done "yesterday." Unfortunately, the seller is constrained by product lead times and inventory, and cannot always meet the customer's deadline. Many salespeople, raised in the "don't confuse selling with delivering" philosophy, just respond "no problem" and then, when the product fails to arrive as promised, they blame it on the factory or the distributor or the freight line. When that no longer works and the customer becomes irate, they switch to avoiding his phone calls. Within his own company, the customer has now lost face and become a victim of the salesperson's failure to set realistic expectations. His only choice now is to blame the vendor, and to tell anyone who will listen that you and your company failed to perform. At this point, unless you are the only company in the world providing a solution to his problem, you can kiss future business good-bye.

If you know you cannot meet the customer's deadline, say so. Chances are pretty good your competition can't either. The soulful response is to brainstorm with the customer about ways to come closer to the deadline. Can you make use of the lead time to begin training staff? Can you loan equipment or a demonstrator model in the interim? Can you get all the wiring and cabling issues addressed and tested ahead of time? Can you split the cost of shipping it overnight air? Be creative and work with her to put together a plan.

If you have reason to believe you can meet the deadline but find out after the sale that you won't, call the customer immediately. Bad news, unlike fine wine, never improves with age. The vinegar taste in your customer's mouth must be acknowledged. Then, turn all your energies to working with him to develop a contingency plan.

We've Decided Not to Do Anything at This Time …

You've just spent six months working with a customer to develop a solution to his problem, and suddenly he's saying, "We've decided not to do anything right now." Since this defies common sense, some salespeople will respond with body language—or even words like, "Are you crazy? Do you know how hard I've worked on this? What are you thinking?"

Do you really believe your customer just led you on a merry dance for six months for the pure hell of it? Don't you suspect she may be every bit as frustrated as you are at this point? Your real need, of course, is not to vent your frustration, but to understand what's behind this statement. You don't want to put your customer on the defensive. You need to summarize where each of you is right now and what is likely to happen in the future.

"Tell me more about what you're thinking. What are some of the reasons you're thinking it's better to wait?" The responses may surprise you. Perhaps what the customer is really saying is that your solution is not convincing. Perhaps she cannot see how your offering can help her really solve her problem. Or she may believe your product will create new and different problems rather than delivering value. Oops. Someone skipped too lightly through the qualifying stage …

Or maybe he's saying that they are going to try to solve it another way using their own staff. Instead of buying your computer program, they're going to "roll their own." When you asked who the competition would be, did you forget to ask whether they were considering a homegrown approach? Were they using you and other vendors just to get an education, all the while preparing to do their own development? If so, there should have been indicators all along that alerted you to probe for more information. If you had reason to believe they might want to develop their own solution, your final proposal should have stressed the many benefits of purchasing your product, your experience, and your expertise at customizing versus starting from scratch to learn about and build a new system.

Maybe what your customer is really saying is that he was unable to sell it to his manager. Or that he couldn't get the funding approved. Oops. There's that darned qualifying thing again. If you determined earlier that funding was approved and available and verified that with more than one source, you would not be in this position. If you had learned it was *not* approved, you would have wisely proceeded with a budgetary proposal first to resolve the issue.

And who is this manager she couldn't "sell" it to? Didn't you learn about him or her earlier? If you didn't or if you failed to make a call on this person both to verify what you were learning and to determine what were the most important benefits to him or her, then you were not ready to present your solution. Worse than that, by not contacting that manager directly, you put your customer in the position of having to sell for you, something which she could not possibly be as good at as you are. You took yourself, your commitment to the customer, and all the work you did to understand the business situation and need right out of the equation and left your customer holding the ball.

Or maybe there has been a serious business downturn and your project has been put on hold. Or funding has temporarily been held up. If that's the case, you and your customer need to establish a follow-up plan. You want to keep your solution uppermost in his mind and be ready to come in and update your proposal when funds are again available. This may mean you talk to him or others at the company once a month, or that you make a phone call to "check in" periodically. It does *not* mean you go away and write on your calendar to call back in six months. Things change rapidly in business, and you may come back to find someone else's product installed because you went away and they didn't. Patience and persistence are two of the qualities we need in these situations.

Selling with soul is remembering we are all human beings, with all the glory and the faults that implies. We bring logic to our decisions, but only after our emotions, wants, biases, and personal histories are already there. We have goals for our business and our job, but also for our personal careers and our political aspirations. We are complex and fascinating, and a sales professional understands and appreciates that.

An old industry joke used to be that "the only difference between a computer salesman and a used car salesman was that the used car salesman *knew* when he was lying." None of us can see the whole picture or all the details at any point in time. Give your customer the benefit of the doubt by believing that he is telling you the truth as he sees it. Assume that he, like you, wants to do the right thing and that he, like you, wants to take pride in his work and himself. When you assume the best about people, you very often get to see and enjoy them at their best.

REFLECTIONS ON CHAPTER 10
Discovering and Responding to Concerns

It is better to suffer wrong than to do it, and happier to be sometimes cheated than not to trust.
—Samuel Johnson

Take a few minutes to evaluate your own ability to discover the customer's concerns and to respond to them. You may need to be an amateur psychologist sometimes to understand what a customer is really saying. The same is true in our ongoing questioning to confirm we are still on the right track toward winning a sale that is mutually beneficial.

1. 1. Are you able to listen to criticism or concerns about your products and services without becoming defensive or arguing with the customer? Are you sure you understand the concern before you reply? Do you paraphrase what you heard to minimize misunderstanding?
2. Are you honest when your product doesn't offer a feature or function that your customer has a real need for? Or do you try to convince him that you'll have it in the next release? It is better to leave the relationship based on honesty than to cross your fingers and hope the feature will really be there soon enough to help.
3. Do you empathize with the customer who is showing nervousness about the risk or the investment being proposed? Do you remind her of the steps she took to make a good decision? Or do you just tell her she shouldn't worry?
4. Have you presented your price honestly and fairly and shown the value the customer can expect to receive as a result of the purchase? If you are careful to ask your customer to quantify what benefit will result, how much time he will save, how much expense he can eliminate, and other key questions about the plan you have developed together, your price is based on what he has identified as his needs. It is not arbitrary, padded, or inflated.

5. Are you ready to negotiate with confidence that you have earned this sale and a commitment that you will deliver on your customer's expectations for a successful implementation?

Figure 7. I earn the business by understanding the concerns and honestly resolving them.

CHAPTER 11

The Importance Of Listening

SOME OLD SAGE SAID that God gave us two ears and one mouth to remind us to listen twice as much as we talk. The stereotype of the salesperson as a "good talker" is sadly off the mark. Professional salespeople are good listeners. By good listeners, I mean more than people who hear and remember what was said. It is equally important to hear what is not being said, to draw out opinions and concerns, and to respectfully question and confirm your understanding of what was said.

A good listener is active and engaged. He is not just waiting for his turn. Most of us find it extremely difficult to sustain active listening. So many obstacles present themselves. For example, we listen at a much faster rate than most people talk, so our brains experience frustration similar to our own impatience when the computer flashes an hourglass icon at us instead of just getting on with it. As a result, we may "get it" long before the other person finishes her sentence, or at least we think we do. Once we think we know what the speaker will say, our brain finishes it for her and then wanders off to explore some other subject of interest, leaving our ears in background mode waiting for the "period" that means it's our turn. Similarly, if the speaker is formulating a question and we believe we know the answer, we become impatient at how long it takes him to ask and often jump in, eager to show him our knowledge.

There are significant differences in how people communicate based on their gender, race, education level, cultural conditioning, regional patterns, and personality style. The more I learn about the many "filters" that affect how we communicate, the more amazed I am that we ever manage to understand each other at all! Selling with empathy requires us to understand and respect differences. It also demands that we know our own "filters" and improve our ability to listen through them.

Many of us are driven, "Type A" personalities, for whom the word "patience" might as well be spelled with only four letters. The "P word" haunts me. I have been given many opportunities in my life to develop patience; sadly, I remain a novice. The universe presents me again and again with the lesson that "things take time." I resist the lesson, and I persist in my futile attempts to control situations, events, and sometimes, people. For years I had an old favorite cartoon hanging in my cubicle. It showed two vultures talking while their counterparts circled. One says to the other, "Patience, hell. Let's just kill something."

For salespeople, lack of patience manifests itself in many ways. We may hurry to finish the customer's sentence for him, eager to show that we understand. We may interrupt a long discourse that seems to be wandering off track and attempt to bring it back to the point—*our* point. We may urge a person to make a decision even though we have not completed all the steps necessary for her to feel comfortable and confident enough to do so.

Patience is respect. Patience is recognizing that we all act, decide, and form conclusions at our own pace. Patience recognizes that we have different comfort zones and different needs for data. The process cannot be rushed nor can it be shortchanged, unless you are willing to risk the customer later feeling resentful at having been pushed. Remember the last time you felt forced into a decision you weren't ready to make. Did you resent the person who urged you to decide? Do you find yourself now distrusting his or her motives?

One important reminder I use to help myself cultivate patience is that "It always takes less time to do things the right way than it takes to fix them after they've been done the wrong way." One of my customers kept a sign in his order processing department with a similar thought: "Why is there never time to do it right but always time to do it over?" Another customer uses an acronym: D.I.R.T.F.T. It stands for "Do it right the first time."

Throughout the selling process, our souls demand the patience to do it right; and when we ignore that demand, we suffer. When ignored, our soul will use our body to get our attention. Headaches, stiff backs, and aching necks are all our soul's way of telling us we are not "right" with ourselves. Adopting the selling with soul philosophy means that we first learn to actively listen to ourselves and to understand our own emotions. We pay attention to how our words and our emotions affect those around us. We may have negative self-talk to overcome and thoughts that do not serve us. We may doubt our abilities or question our actions until the result is an ongoing sense of unease. The late great actress Mercedes McCambridge once said that the reason she drank was that she could not stop comparing her insides with other people's outsides. We need to give ourselves the same understanding and empathy we share with customers. The better we become at listening to ourselves and doing so kindly, the better we become at listening to others.

To quote Susan Scott, author of *Fierce Conversations,* "All conversations are with myself, and sometimes they involve other people ... I may think I see you as you are, but in truth I see you as I am. The implications of this are staggering, and not the least of them is this: The issues in my life are rarely about you. They are almost always about me. This means that I cannot come out from behind myself into conversations with others and make them real until I know who I am and what I intend to do with my life" (p. 83)

For salespeople, gender differences hold special significance. Research done in the seventies and reported by author John Molloy in *Dress for Success* measured the results of sales training programs. The study yielded the surprising information that women were more successful at selling before being trained than they were after completing a formal training program. The results were attributed to the fact that women in our society are taught to listen actively and supportively to others and to build rapport through their speech patterns. This skill allows them to build empathy and to bond more easily with customers. Men, on the other hand, are taught to take a competitive or one-up stance in conversation and are accustomed to challenging each other in speech. Since the formal sales training had been based on male speech patterns, it actually undermined the women's familiar patterns, substituting ill-fitting models of direct and competitive speaking. As a result, the newly trained women appeared uncomfortable to customers and lost credibility.

Sales training programs in the eighties emphasized feature/benefit selling, which involved telling the customer what benefit she could expect to enjoy as a result of a given product feature. In the nineties, the preferred sales model was consultative selling, which incorporated in-depth questioning and understanding of the customer prior to presenting any proposed solution.

Regardless of methodology, the cultural differences that shape how men and women communicate are better understood thanks to researchers like John Gray and Deborah Tannen. John Gray's book *Men Are from Mars, Women Are from Venus* became a best seller based on our strong desire to better understand our partners. He explained to many readers for the first time the "male" pattern of "going into the cave" to unwind, recover, think, rest, and so on, and the "female" pattern of "talking it out." Many of us women laughed as we recognized ourselves and our own futile attempts to chase a man out of his cave so we could talk. In her book *You Just Don't Understand,* Deborah Tannen, PhD, gives many examples of miscommunication in a business environment that are the result of gender differences in communication patterns. Two examples are:

1. Men declaim while women question. Men will often make statements even if they are not certain that what they are asserting is true. They state their opinion with confidence and wait for the response. Women more often express their opinion as a question, or even if it is posed as a statement, raise their vocal inflection at the end of the statement so that a questioning tone is conveyed. Many of us, both men and women, react predictably to these patterns. Reacting to the confidence in the man's tone, we assume that his statement is based on a well-researched conclusion or authoritative opinion. Similarly, we perceive a lack of confidence in the female speaker and hesitate to accept her statement. The man may be bluffing. The woman may not want to seem pushy. Nonetheless, we react to how they speak rather than to what they say. It is important that we ask respectful questions and ascertain the difference. To be fooled by style is a common mistake of rookie salespeople. Going beneath the "fluff" to measure the "stuff" is essential.

A good example of this in our personal lives would be a woman asking her husband, "Are you hungry?" and him answering "no." He heard her words, but not their intent, which was a "female" way of saying, "I'm hungry. How about if we get something to eat?" Many of us can think of arguments that began with little misunderstandings of this type.

2. Women "vent" while men "fix." My husband still needs me to tell him whether I am describing a situation just to "get it off my chest" or

whether I am looking for advice or help in solving it. Many times I've become irritated with him because he starts busily making suggestions intended to solve "my problem," when all I really wanted was for him to listen and make sympathetic "mm hmms" once in a while so I feel I've been heard. When he responds to venting with phrases like, "Have you tried …?" or "Why don't you …?" it has the same effect on me as biting into aluminum foil. Instead of feeling heard, I feel patronized or put-down, and my temper flares. He, of course, only means to be helpful and assumes that if I'm talking about an issue to him, I must be interested in his opinion and his help. To his credit, he now waits for me to finish speaking and then asks, "Is this the one where I'm supposed to say, 'I hear you, baby,' or is this the one where I'm supposed to say, 'What have you done about this so far?'"

In the face of gender differences, we are all challenged to become bilingual. As business becomes more diverse, both male and female salespeople will need to hone this skill to be true professionals.

Regional differences are another challenge. I once gave a presentation on our company's global network on how to sell to information technology professionals. These technical buyers were sometimes seen as adversaries by our own sales. The sales engineers for whom I had developed the talk had much in common. For the most part, they were white men with four-year engineering degrees, were single or had a wife who was not employed outside the home, had played sports in college, voted Republican, and golfed in the nineties. My talk had originally been a one-hour class that included some interactive work with the sales engineers in my home district. For the purposes of the broadcast, however, I had to get it down to thirty minutes and eliminate the exercises. After much painstaking editing, I managed to do so, and after the broadcast, I was gratified to receive a number of calls from my peers around the country thanking me for providing a valuable tutorial. When I picked up the phone and heard my counterpart in Dallas say hello, I grinned, expecting more kudos. He said, "Do you know what my sales engineers said after your segment?" I waited for the expected compliment. "They said: Daa-ang! She-ee taa-lks fa-ast!" So much for believing all sales engineers listen and learn the same way. Despite all the surface similarities, regional differences in communication were a real factor in how much of my "lesson" could be processed in Dallas.

When I spoke or attended customer meetings in New York, I faced the opposite problem. Having grown up in the Midwest, I tended to speak what Garrison Keillor calls "Minnesotan," the essence of which is accommodating, inoffensive language, passive construction, and statements in the form of a question. It is not polite to be direct in the Midwest. A request like "fill 'er up" shouted out a rolled-down window at a gas station would be considered so rude as to be offensive. The more Midwestern approach would sound something like, "Hi. How are you? Good. If you're not too busy, would you mind filling it up when you have a minute?" In New York, the land of "take a breath and lose your turn," such an approach would brand you as a rube or someone with the IQ of a philodendron.

My husband grew up in Brooklyn and has no difficulty confronting rude clerks, inefficient service providers, or other annoying people. I still struggle with clearly expressing what I want and holding firm. Not long ago, my husband had a good laugh when I reported the results of my "confrontation" with a rude clerk. When he asked me what I said, I told him I "really told him off" in true Midwesterner fashion. He laughed, knowing that meant I rolled my eyes to the sky and breathed a heavy sigh, while shaking my head in disgust. Boy. Guess I showed him, huh?

Regional differences apply to selling in many ways beyond speech patterns. In the South and in the Northwest, developing the relationship is a prerequisite to doing business together. In Chicago, despite being technically in the Midwest, business is primary, and if we come to like each other in addition, that's just a nice bonus. The salesperson with soul understands these differences and also appreciates the fact that "you can take the boy out of the country, but you can't take the country out of the boy," meaning many of us carry our regional style with us wherever we go. Our careers may take us to Brooklyn, but if we grew up in Chattanooga, Tennessee, we are going to bring along with us a preference for polite and more personal conversation conducted at a slower pace.

Misunderstandings are easily fostered by failures to appreciate differences in communication style between racial and ethnic groups. My first experience with this came when interviewing a group of sales training candidates that included two African American men. Both had grown up in southern states and had graduated from well-respected engineering schools. After the interviews, some of my colleagues questioned whether what they saw as "poor eye contact" might indicate the candidates were not confident enough for a career in sales. When the human resources manager pointed out that we might be seeing a racial or cultural difference, I had an "aha" moment. What is considered respectful and appropriate in one region or culture may be interpreted in a completely different way somewhere else. While Southerners in general are brought up to speak softly and indirectly, this polite style does not indicate a lack of confidence or strength. The movie *Steel Magnolias* showed a strength of will and character beneath a genteel exterior that should never be underestimated.

Many such examples can be found. Selling with empathy means taking the time to learn the context and the background of our customers, as well as understanding how our own backgrounds influence our thinking. Southern regional speech patterns or African-American dialect may be "heard" as uneducated or unintelligent, reflecting a northern or white bias. The fast-clipped cadences of New York and New Jersey may be heard as arrogant and argumentative. The many viewers of the movie *Fargo* may have found themselves thinking the self-effacing characters, who spoke fluent "Minnesotan," were a little slow and dim-witted. Part of the movie's appeal is our pleasant surprise and growing admiration for the female sheriff as we follow her wise, perceptive, and persistent efforts to solve the murder.

Differences as basic as how close we stand to each other and whether we are more comfortable talking side by side or face-to-face must be taken into account. Women prefer talking face-to-face, while men are often seen talking side by side, whether walking or seated. North Americans stand farther apart than South Americans. Punctuality means something totally different with Northern Europeans than it does with Southern Europeans. The list is endless.

All these factors come into play as we form and manage our relationships. And managing our relationships is at the heart of professional selling. Historically there has been great pressure on individuals within business to fit the mold. Homogeneity of style has been forced, and assimilation has been the norm when different cultures and backgrounds came together. Today's business climate, however, is increasingly diverse, and it will be important for the sales professional to increase his or her own tolerance for differences. Avoiding stereotypes, while at the same time appreciating differences in training, upbringing, and perspective, is part of selling with soul.

The following summary is from the Internet site www.familycare.org. It helps put the importance of respecting diversity in perspective for me as well as helping me remember to be grateful for my many blessings:

If the population of the world were reduced to one village of precisely 100 people, with all the existing human ratios remaining the same, it would look like this:

- The village would have 61 Asians, 13 Africans, 12 Europeans, 9 Latin Americans, and 5 from the USA and Canada.
- 50 would be male, 50 would be female.
- 75 would be non-white; 25 white.
- 67 would be non-Christian; 33 would be Christian.
- 80 would live in substandard housing.
- 16 would be unable to read or write.
- 50 would be malnourished and 1 dying of starvation.
- 33 would be without access to a safe water supply.
- 39 would lack access to improved sanitation.
- 24 would not have any electricity. (And of the 76 that do have electricity, most would only use it for light at night.)
- 8 people would have access to the Internet.
- 1 would have a college education.
- 1 would have HIV.
- 2 would be near birth; 1 near death.
- 5 would control 32% of the entire world's wealth; all 5 would be US citizens.
- 48 would live on less than US$ 2 a day.
- 20 would live on less than US$ 1 a day.

Becoming a Better Listener

There are many things you can read to help you understand your own filters and biases. Becoming a better listener, however, depends on practice. Here are some ideas you may want to try to improve your own listening abilities.

1. After a sales call, take a few moments to ask yourself the following:
    - Did I talk more than I listened?
    - Did I interrupt?
    - Did I ask questions patiently and wait to hear the full answer?
    - Did I notice changes in body language?

- Did my own attention wander?
- Did I remember to restate what I heard as the customer's position before I disagreed with it?
- Did I remember to summarize at the end of the discussion and make sure the customer agreed with the summary?

2. In the next meeting you attend, make it a point to do the following:
   - Resist the temptation to sort papers or go through your mail.
   - Put your smartphone away and notice how many people hide theirs under the desk and do the "smartphone prayer" pose, believing no one notices.
   - Watch to see if others have side conversations, and resist the temptation to do so yourself.
   - Monitor your body language for signs of impatience: finger tapping, sighing, and so on.
   - After each presentation, see if you can summarize the main point in one or two sentences.

Becoming a good listener is essential to becoming a good communicator. Selling with soul demands that we sharpen our listening skills and use them with empathy for ourselves and others.

REFLECTIONS ON CHAPTER 11
The Importance of Listening

The right word may be effective, but no word was ever as effective as a rightly timed pause.
—Mark Twain

The following questions are designed to help you identify your strengths and weaknesses in listening. Take some time to work through them.

1. Do I often have disagreements with my customers or coworkers based on their saying they told me something and I did not remember it?
2. Does my partner complain that I don't listen?
3. Do I often catch my attention wandering when I'm trying to listen to a presentation?
4. Do I interrupt others?
5. Am I so eager to make my point that I finish someone else's sentence?
6. Enlist a partner and improve your comprehension by summarizing, not parroting, to each other what you hear in conversation. Getting feedback can help you improve. Some questions to ask of others are:
   - Did you feel you had my attention?
   - Did I seem impatient or restless when you were speaking?
   - Are there things I can do to make it clear I am hearing and understanding you?

Note to Self: Remember to listen with empathy.

CHAPTER 12

The "Close" And Why It's Really The Opening

LET'S JUST GET RID of the term *closing*. Let's call it what it is: asking for and receiving the order. I don't know where the term *close the sale* originated—perhaps with J. Douglas Edwards, who is known as the "father of closing"—but it is an oxymoron. Asking for the order is the opening of a relationship at a higher level, not the closing of one, and the term *close* smacks of springing a trap or catching the customer unaware. The whole image is abhorrent to those of us who sell with soul.

Most sales training books will handle the "closing" section by providing sample questions or scripts. They will tell you it is better to say, "Shall we go over the paperwork?" than "Are you ready to sign?" Certain words will be identified as red flags or "stop signs" that may put a customer off or make him hesitant to proceed.

"Shall we go ahead?" is preferred to "Sign here."

"How will you pay for this?" is a no-no since the cost may cause anxiety.

To eliminate buyer anxiety and skip right to the signing, many training books offer magic formulas. For example, the alternate-of-choice close: "Would you prefer to purchase this equipment as a capital expenditure? Or is it better for you if we put together an operating lease?" While it sounds like two questions, picking either one results in a "yes."

Salespeople pay millions of dollars every year to learn the "secrets" of closing and buy books with "proven" scripts and rules. Perhaps the most basic of these is "golden silence," a rule developed by J. Douglas Edwards and taught as simply: Whenever you ask a closing question, shut up. The first person to speak loses. Notice the winner versus loser approach, which has already been discussed and which has been out of style with customers and salespeople alike since the 1970s.

More sophisticated examples have been taught to thousands of salespeople by trainers like Tom Hopkins, who in his *How to Master the Art of Selling* lists "Twelve Power Closes for Aspiring Champions," starting with "the basic oral close." He instructs you to ask, "Which purchase order number" will be assigned, and when they say they don't know, "smile and say, 'Why don't we find out?'" He includes scripts, such as "My Dear Old Mother," which advises you to quote your mother, or someone else's, as having taught you, "Silence implies consent"; the magic question is followed by a flash of your winning smile and the follow-on question, "Was she right?" Hopkins, of course, emphasizes that if your mother never said this, you must go to her and ask her to state this to you verbatim; otherwise, you would be lying—and we wouldn't want to do that. How do customers respond to this behavior? Do they look back on the experience as a satisfying exchange? Or do they experience buyer's remorse?

Research done by Neil Rackham and published in his book *SPIN Selling (page 36)* showed that customers who have been aggressively "closed" are less satisfied than those who were not. When asking 145 customers three to five days after purchase to rate their satisfaction with the goods purchased and the likelihood of making a similar purchase in the future from the same store, strong "closing" proved a liability. Those who had detected being "closed" rated their satisfaction as 5.8 on a scale of 10 and their likelihood to purchase again at 5.2. Those who had *not* perceived closing behavior in the course of the transaction rated their satisfaction at 7.7 and their likelihood to purchase at 7.9.

When you sell with soul, you have logically proceeded through the steps, identifying mutual agreement and mutual benefit along the way, and there is no clear-cut shift to closing. Rather, you may find yourself discussing the implementation plan or timing in detail once it is clear that the customer is ready to proceed. Simple questions along the way like, "Are we on track?" and "Have I missed anything?" combined with regular reviews of what you and the customer have agreed to so far, provide the opportunity to make a midcourse correction if you are no longer in agreement. That can happen at any time in a presentation, a discussion of concerns, or planning for a successful implementation. When you are checking in with your customer, making sure you agree on both the direction and the method of travel; there is no need to shove her through a door and "close" it at the end of the journey.

Once the customer has given you a verbal purchase order, agreeing that you are the vendor of choice, there is still a lot of work to be done. Before you break out the champagne, break out your notebook and confirm one more time that you and the customer are in agreement on scope, timetable, and other details. You must confirm verbally that what you believe you are "selling" and what the customer believes he is "buying" are one and the same, and then follow up in writing.

When the customer says "yes," the sales professional with soul hears it as "I'm trusting you to prove your integrity and to deliver on your promise." If instead of feeling gratified at having earned the customer's trust, your stomach begins to hurt, go back and look at whether you may have overcommitted or overstated the value you intend to deliver. Your body's response is your soul knowing you've been less than truthful, even if you have not consciously chosen to "lie." One of the greatest of human skills is the ability to rationalize, and we all want to be right and to be able to defend our choices and behaviors. Our consciences may not always be loud enough to be heard by our inner ear, but our bodies will usually give us feedback when our behavior or our decisions are not consistent with our principles. The cartoons of the little angel on one shoulder and the little devil on the other would be more accurate if they depicted the little devil as an ulcer, a migraine, or a sudden attack of irritable bowel syndrome. Selling with soul requires that we avoid rationalization.

When you ask for the order, be certain you want it. This requires that you have an implementation plan and that you and your customer both understand and agree on how you will determine whether you delivered as promised. If you have based your summary of benefits on reducing downtime by 10 percent because of your product's high meantime between failure data, then your customer will not be satisfied with a 5 percent reduction, even if that amounts to a substantial savings. Psychologists use the term "cognitive dissonance" for the gap between what we expect and what we experience. Salespeople who exaggerate or who persuade based on the "trust me—it's going to be wonderful" message are setting their customers up for a severe case of buyer's remorse, and they will pay the price later in lost credibility and future opportunities.

If you have sold your product as a tool for increasing output or throughput, you and your customer will have an expectation of how many more units will be produced or how much less time will be needed to produce a number of units equal to today's output. Again, set the expectation properly. If you exceed the customer's expectations, you have demonstrated greater value than promised, and your own credibility rises as a result. If you fail to meet the expectations you set or if you allow the customer to set expectations that you know are unrealistic or rely on factors you cannot control, you have created a no-win scenario for both the customer and yourself.

Many salespeople grab that purchase order and run back to their offices to get it entered. Once it is in the system and they know it will show up on their commission report, contact with the customer becomes unimportant to them. In fact, if the customer calls them, they may hand the call off to an installer or service specialist. This hit-and-run method of selling is a significant contributor to the distrust that many customers bring with them into the buying process.

Selling with soul means that you have agreed on expectations and agreed on metrics that will be used to determine whether or not they have been met, and that you have continued to demonstrate your commitment to deliver on your promise. Some of the ways you do this are:

Remember to say thank you. Most of us will shake hands with a warm smile and say thank you for the order at the time that we receive it. Use your empathy for a moment. When you buy something, you enjoy a brief period of delight. You have made your decision and will soon be enjoying the benefits of your purchase. Within a day or two of the decision, however, we begin second-guessing ourselves. This human tendency is so common that many states have laws allowing a three-day cooling-off period. During this time, the buyer can change her mind, cancel a contract, or return a purchase with no penalty. It is during this period that your customer will most appreciate your thank you. A note from you that thanks him for the confidence he has placed in you and reminds him of some of the benefits he will soon see will be appreciated—and reassuring. In the business world, feeling appreciated and being reassured are rare experiences for most of us, and yet they are basic human needs.

Keep the information flow going. Once the order has been entered, the customer expects to see an order acknowledgment and a promise date. Few things are more frustrating for the customer than waiting weeks on end for something to cross her desk that shows progress on delivery. Once you have acknowledged the order, providing a sales order number or a tracking number for his reference and you have provided a promise date, make sure you correct and update this information if it should change. Many customers have told me that a product shipping late is only a small problem if they know it will be late. They can usually do some contingency planning and minimize the impact. But a product being late as a surprise, or not finding out about the delay until it was expected on the receiving dock, is a *big* problem. At that point, it is too late for them to recoup the time lost.

Rather than doing everything in your power to avoid being the bearer of bad news, you have an opportunity to show respect for your customer's time and process. Go ahead and be the messenger. The likelihood she will shoot you is small. Tell her. Tell it straight. Tell it as soon as you know. If she needs to vent some frustration, take it. It's never fatal. Get it over with and get on with the contingency planning.

The better you get to know your customer, the more ways you will find to be of service. Account management is a continuous learning process and, like any relationship, requires that you pay attention. After winning a sale and seeing the implementation through, one of the most educational exercises for both you and your customer is the post-installation meeting. This is your opportunity to verify and to learn by asking questions like the following:

- Do you agree that the solution is now in place and performing to your expectations? Is there anything left to be done or that remains an open issue?
- Were there any surprises along the way that we should have anticipated? How could we have avoided them? How will we make sure we do better on the next project?
- Was there anything you wish we had done differently?

Discussions like this should be open and candid, with the goal of improvement in mind. If there is dissatisfaction with how things went, it is important to allow the customer to express that and to listen without defensiveness or interruptions. Then, once the emotion has been aired, open up the discussion to brainstorming ways to avoid mistakes in the future.

When you approach each step of the sales cycle as a listening and learning opportunity, you deepen the relationship and help the customer feel confident about working with you in the future. He may also be willing to do something helpful to you, such as provide a reference.

When you have done a good job for your customer, go ahead and ask if he or she would be willing to provide a reference for you. Many times new customers will want to talk to someone who has worked with you before, and having the names and phone numbers of your satisfied customers will answer their need to verify what you are telling them. Never give out a customer's name or phone number without asking first if he is willing to be contacted. Respect her time and her demanding schedule by discussing it with her well beforehand. Once he agrees, though, you have a testimonial that can put you far ahead of the competition and open up opportunities for you that seemed out of reach.

When you have been given the opportunity to work with a customer, to solve her problem, to earn his trust, you have formed a relationship. Relationships require maintenance. Check back in with the customer from time to time to make certain things are still going well. Check back to see if there are future business opportunities. Check back just to see if the customer is healthy and happy. A brief phone call, even a warm message on voice mail, lets the customer know that he or she is a person, not just a paycheck, and that you are more concerned about winning a customer than about winning a commission.

Our lives are faster-paced than ever before, and each day we are bombarded with more information than we could ever comprehend or use. For professional salespeople, learning must be a lifelong commitment. To bring knowledge and experience to our customers, we must be constantly on the lookout for new and valuable ideas and information. To that end, we cannot afford to be afraid of change or to shrink from new technology. The Chinese spell *crisis* with a combination of two characters, one representing "danger" and the other representing "opportunity." The greatest danger in any crisis may well be failing to see the opportunity. Abraham Lincoln once said that, "Opportunity often knocks disguised as hard work. As a result, most people fail to recognize it."

There is little we can do to slow the pace of change or the roller coaster of technological advances, so we may as well enjoy the ride. As salespeople with soul, we need to embrace change and recognize that every new situation presents a learning opportunity if we are open to it. To be the best we can be, each of us needs challenge. We all need to stretch and enlarge our comfort zones by doing the things we fear and giving ourselves permission to make mistakes. If we do, we learn and grow, in increments, one step at a time, and we become our own personal best.

REFLECTIONS ON CHAPTER 12
The "Close" and Why It's Really the Opening

The customer doesn't expect everything will go right all the time; the big test is what you do when things go wrong.
—Sir Colin Marshall

The following questions are intended to help you win the order and be confident that the customer will be pleased with the result. Although some companies hire "hunters" and then turn over account management responsibilities to someone on the inside as soon as an order is won, the salesperson with soul recognizes that a relationship has been established and continues to pay attention to it, perhaps not at the same level of intensity but in ways that matter to the customer.

1. Have you allowed the time for your customer to complete his evaluation without pressure? Is he in agreement that the product or service you recommend will help him solve his business problem or achieve his goal?

2. Are the steps in your evaluation sequence all complete? Has anything been skipped that may come back to cause problems later?

3. Have you helped your customer identify the value of the proposed solution and the cost of leaving the problem unsolved? Has your customer agreed with the estimates of cost versus benefit?

4. Have you had a discussion about implementation with the person who will be responsible for overseeing it? Have you offered services where they can be beneficial?

5. Are you prepared to negotiate, confident of the value you have identified with the customer and proud of the work you have done to get to this point? Have you identified what you will ask the customer to do for you before you do anything else for her?

Figure 8. Once you have earned the business, the salesperson with soul continues to earn the customer's confidence that he or she made the right decision.

CHAPTER 13

Managing Growth Through Conflict

CONFLICT IS A FACT of life. How we respond to it is a choice. Our reactions to conflict vary and are influenced by our upbringing and our personality. I grew up in a family that considered a spirited argument, complete with yelling and sometimes name-calling, to be normal conversation. My best friend grew up in a family that never raised their voices. She frequently sees "conflict" where I see only passion, and what energizes me can be stressful for her. Sales professionals encounter conflict at home and on the job, with customers, coworkers, production, finance, and more. Selling with soul requires that we become expert at recognizing and addressing conflict. It begins with understanding our own reactions to conflict.

Conflict produces adrenaline, also known as the "fight, flight, or freeze" response. If you are a "fighter," you will react to conflict by wanting to jump in, arguing your position and trying to get the better of your opponent. Some of us even become adrenaline junkies and will pick a fight just to liven things up when life feels a little too stable. The expression "winning the battle but losing the war" should help us understand that if we focus on winning a fight, we may very well lose an opportunity.

If you have the "flight" response, you will either find ways to avoid the situation and the conflict or you will assume the role of peacemaker, trying to bring everyone together in a happy resolution of the differences. This is not always possible because real differences exist among our agendas and our priorities. Pushing for compromise may result in everyone feeling they lost.

If you "freeze" in the face of conflict, you may change the subject or pretend not to hear the concerns being presented. You may even find yourself shutting down, unable to think creatively or to see a way out of the situation.

While we may not be able to change our immediate limbic reaction to conflict, we can and must choose *how* we respond. Rethinking some basic assumptions can help. For example, conflict is *not* negative. Conflict is, in fact, necessary for any positive change to occur. The comfort of doing something in an old, familiar way versus the opportunity to do it differently and better creates conflict. We need to see it as a learning opportunity rather than a problem.

Conflict is *not* one person being right and another being wrong. Conflict is difference. Resolving it usually involves new information and a rethinking of the viewpoints involved, rather than having one side proclaimed "the winner."

And, finally, conflict is *not* usually about personalities, despite many people's tendencies to write off any disagreement as a "personality conflict." It usually involves goals or desired outcomes that seem to be mutually exclusive. Once you focus on the goals rather than the personalities, it becomes easier to find a solution.

Fighters have a strong desire to win and see every conflict situation as a chance to come out on top. The real problem is that the other party has to then be pushed to the bottom. No organization since feudalism has benefited for long with this scenario. If you are a fighter, your learning opportunity is to transcend the dualistic view of conflict and train yourself to look for the synthesis or collaboration that can result when you treat the other viewpoint as a lesson instead of a threat. This is not the same thing as compromise. Rather, it means collaboration and redefining the "win."

For example, if Bob and Judy both have a major sales proposal due and are in conflict over the amount of time they get from the departmental secretary, Pat, it would do no good to say that in the interests of fairness, Pat would spend four hours on each proposal. Especially if both proposals are due tomorrow and each will take six hours to complete. In this instance, both Bob and Judy lose.

Nor would it make sense to say Bob got there first so Judy's out of luck. If both Bob and Judy are fighters, they'll argue vehemently that their proposal is more important to the company than the other's, and poor Pat will be stuck right in the middle. If one of them is a "flighter," he or she may stalk off, refusing to fight, and either stay up all night trying to do the proposal without help or walk away from the opportunity. That scenario will not only cost the department a potential sale, but possibly a fine sales representative, who becomes resentful and decides down the road that he or she is not valued.

While fighters let everyone know they are upset, sometimes causing stress to anyone within shouting distance, flighters take a significant toll on the organization as well when they hide or avoid conflict. If they give in, they will surely become resentful at some point. A resentful employee affects the morale of the whole team and eventually leaves voluntarily or is let go, as his performance worsens in direct proportion to his attitude. If he avoids the conflict and finds temporary ways around it, the situation remains unresolved and may eventually become explosive. At the same time, the potential for learning and for process improvement that comes along with almost any conflict is lost to the organization.

Conflict can be beneficial and a powerful motivator for change. The first rule, however, is to attack the problem, not the people. Separate the issues from the personalities. Being able to hear the worthwhile points in Fighting George's position, even though he's bugged you ever since he got promoted and started acting so cocky, is difficult. Being able to patiently extract the details of Flighty Fred's concerns, even though he keeps glancing at the door and trying to change the subject, is challenging. The first and most essential step, however, is being able to list the goals and desired outcomes associated with each position.

At this stage, it often becomes apparent that people have the same goal in mind but very different ideas as to how to achieve it. If, in fact, the goals themselves are in conflict, it might be necessary to reexamine the directives given to each person in order to determine how they resulted in mutually exclusive goals in the first place.

If there are some common goals to build from, the conflict may be one of resources. Anything is possible given enough money and time, but I have yet to work in a company with unlimited money or time. As a result, my top priority commands my resources, and that may mean that your top priority has to wait. We are often so enamored of our own position that the views of another person sound idiotic to us. Or, perhaps, we think she is just uninformed, so we launch into repeated explanations of our own position, barraging her with the "facts" as we see them. Contrast that behavior with how we react when we believe the other person is intelligent or has expertise we lack. In that case, we ask questions, listen, and try to understand. In Susan Scott's excellent book *Fierce Conversations,* she describes it this way:

"The fundamental outcome of most communication is misunderstanding. We all just attended the same different meeting or participated in the same different conversation. No matter what a person says, we decide in the privacy of our minds what he or she really means by it and then operate as if our interpretation is true, without checking it out. He said this. You heard that. You intended one thing; however, the recipient of your message gave your words a meaning that never even crossed your mind. How many times have you said to someone, "I wish we had tape-recorded our conversation because it would prove that I never said …" or "that I *did* say …"? Each of you was convinced your interpretation was the right one." (p.178)

A worthwhile exercise is to have each person reverse positions and argue for the other side for a set amount of time. If they cannot do so convincingly, they have not really understood the position. Stop. Ask questions. Get clarification. Try it again. Once both sides can fairly state the position of the other, they lose the fear that they are not being heard and are better able to seek common ground and possible solutions.

Physics teaches us that every action has an opposite and equal reaction. This could also be called a law of sociology or biology, because nowhere is it more apparent than in interactions between people. My first temptation when I began to see myself as a leader for change was to confront every issue, whenever and wherever I could. This is no more than the business equivalent of nagging. How do you feel when someone nags at you, especially when, in your heart, you agree with him that your behavior should change? If your spouse gets on you about ordering the French fries or having dessert, do you smile sweetly and thank her for her support? There is a big gap between what we believe we want and what we are truly ready, willing, and able to do at any particular time.

When my husband "shoulds" me, my automatic response is one I've nicknamed "the brat." I sum it up as, "I'll show him. I'll hurt me." I become more stuck in my behaviors than before and go from being defensive on the subject to feeling downright righteous about my right to exercise free will. Of course, I am the loser in this exchange, but in some ways, so is my husband, because at that point we are not communicating. We are just acting out old patterns. All the adult learning and the wisdom we've acquired over the years is temporarily unavailable to us and sits collecting dust, like the exercise equipment in the corner of the bedroom. We would both benefit by communicating with empathy, trying to understand the other person's position and concerns and gently being as clear as we can about our own.

Confrontation, while it may feel just, will polarize the very people we want to reach. It forces them to defend their position and makes it harder for them to consider alternatives. If, instead, we pose the issue and the choices as we understand them and ask for their views, we have opened up a possible dialogue. If we say, "How could you do that?" we have not asked a question at all. We have made a judgment and changed the punctuation. But, if we ask real questions rather than rhetorical ones, allowing for open-ended responses, we make learning possible. And, as we learn, we increase our ability to see potential solutions.

I have met few people in my business career—or in my life—who were just plain mean. I am convinced that the great majority of us prefer doing the right thing to causing harm, and being respected to being feared. Change leaders give everyone the benefit of the doubt. We don't approach others believing they have developed a harmful product or promoted an unethical choice out of a desire to harm others. There is no "Dr. Evil" in my company, and I doubt there is one in yours. But there are people who think they have no choices or who have not looked past the immediate need to reach a goal to examine the long-term ramifications of their decisions. Change leaders help them see that there are always choices and that every choice has a consequence.

Sadly enough, every organization has had experience with people who lie, blame, manipulate, and posture. I wish I could say that they will be punished for such behavior, but the truth is that it may not happen soon enough to satisfy me—or you. While I am a firm believer that "what goes around, comes around," I've also learned that this world doesn't turn on my timetable. Sometimes outright scoundrels get promoted, recognized, and rewarded, and no one seems to notice the trail of broken bodies they left behind them. At those times, all we can do is hold true to our principles and practice our own best behavior, trusting that when we do, we make the world of business a little bit better.

We do not, however, have to be victimized by these people directly. If you are dealing with a liar, make sure you put everything in writing, including your position and desired objectives, so it cannot be easily distorted. The same rule applies to a blamer. Make sure the tone of your communications is factual and not emotional. You might want to make it a rule to print it and let it sit overnight before you send or give it to another person. If you have a tendency like I do to start off telling the facts and to end up venting my frustration, the twenty-four-hour rule is a lifesaver. And, in the heat of the moment, don't use e-mail. There are few more sinking feelings than hitting the send button on impulse, as if you were punctuating a sentence, only to realize that your unchecked, unedited feelings are now being flung to the far corners of the company network.

Manipulators are tough to deal with, unless you have become skilled at smiling and saying no in the nicest possible way. Often they put us in a position where we look (and feel) like hard, uncaring people if we do not cooperate with their requests or their plans. Until you get good at saying no, it is extremely helpful to practice, "I'll get back to you on that." Don't be afraid to sound like you have a one-phrase vocabulary when they keep restating their request. Just smile and say, "I can't give you an answer right now, but I'll get back to you on that."

People who posture do so for power. Whether it is the moral high ground or the political position they are after, they strike a pose and do a convincing act for anyone willing to be their audience. They are often adept at taking credit for the work of others, and of course, if you did most of the work, it is natural to speak up and assert yourself. Sadly, they then get to graciously acknowledge your contribution while you look desperate for attention. The best to be said for these folks is that they usually don't stay around very long. The worst is that they might become your boss.

While it takes two people to create a conflict, it can be resolved by the leadership of one. Whether the differences are between you and your customer, or you and your coworkers, or you and your family, there are five steps you can take to resolve the conflict in a way that is beneficial:

1. First, define the problem. Separating the problem from the people describing it is a necessary first step to seeking the best outcome. Make sure everyone involved agrees on the problem definition. This may mean drawing out the "flighters" or toning down the "fighters," but everyone must agree on what the problem is before they can hope to agree on a solution.
2. Identify the goal or objective being sought by each person involved. This can be tricky, since there are stated goals and

unstated goals, and they can run the full gamut of economic, political, or personal objectives. As the facilitator, you need to make sure that people's words and their body language match and that each person is putting his or her goal on the table. Stating your own goal as honestly as possible is a start. For example, you may state, "I want a full-time sales assistant so I can increase my productivity and my income." Another sales representative may have the same goal. So be it. Making sure everyone understands the "win," for themselves and others, makes it easier to brainstorm without hidden agendas getting in the way.
3. Brainstorm ways to solve the problem. Remember, the rules of brainstorming are simple, but must be enforced: No judging of an idea at the time it is offered. No feedback. No limits. No idea in brainstorming is stupid. Each one will generate several others. The desired outcome is to have as many as possible and to keep the creative juices, and possibly the humor, flowing.
4. As a group, look at the proposed solutions and discuss the pros and cons of each. You will begin to prioritize as you go through this process.
5. Consensus is the best outcome here, with everyone feeling they participated, were heard, and had their goals taken into account before the decision was made. There are times, however, when no consensus is possible, and a decision will have to be made for the good of the company. Your task at those times is to lead with enthusiasm, accepting whatever sacrifice or contribution you need to make and encouraging others to do the same. Make sure you don't participate in or encourage ruminating after the decision is reached. Nothing is accomplished by revisiting it. Move on and encourage others to do the same.

Remember, conflict is inevitable, but how we respond to it is a choice. As change leaders in our organizations, as sellers who approach our customers with soul, and as caring human beings who seek Bob's balance in our family lives, we have an opportunity when presented with conflict. This is our chance to demonstrate our commitment to integrity, ethics, and empathy—in other words, selling with soul.

REFLECTIONS ON CHAPTER 13
Managing Growth through Conflict

Nothing is settled until it is settled right.
—Louis Dembitz Brandeis

How we handle conflict is a true test of our commitment to living a principled life and conducting ourselves as professionals who sell with soul. The questions below can help you look in the mirror and make changes where you are not happy with what you see.

1. When I face conflict, do I fight, take flight, or freeze?
2. When someone disagrees with my position, do I feel devalued as a person? Do I try to understand why he disagrees, or just write off his views as stupid?
3. When I hear someone take an opposing position to my own, do I lie or exaggerate my facts to strengthen my position?
4. Do I hold a grudge against someone long after the conflict is resolved?
5. Am I guilty of putting someone else down to make myself look better?

Note to Self: Remember Stephen Covey's advice and "Seek first to understand, and then to be understood."

CHAPTER 14

Temptations And Compromising Situations

WE DO IT, OUR customers do it, our friends and families do it. And most of us do not consider a politely softened statement or "white lie" to be a falsehood. Such niceties are intended to smooth out the bumps and turns in the road of relationships and avoid the jarring pothole that would hurt another's feelings. Nonetheless, these statements, when used in the practice of professional selling, are potential accidents waiting to happen.

The salesperson seeking to build fast rapport may toss out an innocuous false compliment on the client's appearance, clothing, or office decor. After all, what's the harm? We've all heard ourselves say somewhat hollowly, "Your hair looks great that way" or "You look great—have you lost weight?" Sometimes it draws a pleased smile, but equally often a furrowed brow and an annoyed face are the result. Why? Unless you truly admire the subject at hand and have reason to believe the customer shares your view and takes pride in it as well, you may have inadvertently opened up an old wound. Perhaps the customer just got the worst haircut of her life and has spent the whole morning hoping nobody really notices it until she can get it redone. Or the customer looked into the mirror this morning and finally faced the fact that he's been carrying an extra twenty pounds on his midsection. He's been telling himself all morning that at least he wears it well and few people are aware he is overweight. Along you come with your little well-meaning attempts at building rapport, and you make the haircut or the weight the first thing you mention. So much for the customer's attempts at denial.

Or perhaps you're smarter than to make your opening remarks personal. You look around the customer's office and mention how attractive the glass and chrome conference table is, and the customer almost snarls: "This furniture? I can't stand it. It was picked out by my predecessor, and I'm stuck with it for now." Only later do you realize your customer is a traditionalist, more at home with mahogany and leather office furnishings than anything sleek and contemporary. Now, of course, you have portrayed yourself as a lover of contemporary furnishings, and instead of building rapport, you have a difference in taste to overcome. The error is even more serious if you hate contemporary furniture yourself, because insincerity is almost always detected on some level, even if it is not consciously tagged. An excellent sales trainer I work with calls this the "nice fish" routine, referring to a salesperson's tendency to take something in the room, a mounted fish, for example, and latch onto it as a way to establish rapport. A "nice fish" might get you thirty minutes of your customer reliving the glory of "landing the big guy," or it might get you classified as smarmy and quickly expose the fact that you don't know a muskie from an eel.

It is far better to let rapport evolve as you discover mutual interests and identify common objectives than to try to force it into a business setting. Open your meeting with a sincere statement like, "I'm glad you could meet with me this morning." Of course you are glad! You may have spent a month trying to get this appointment. Go ahead and express your thanks, and then get on with why you're there.

Humor, like beauty, is in the eye of the beholder. I will never understand why some people laugh hysterically at jokes about leprosy or quadriplegics, and yet both subjects have had their day in pop culture, passing through crowds as fast as a virus on a sneeze. Jokes, or other attempts at humor, require you to know your audience thoroughly and well. I once thought elephant jokes to be the height of sophisticated humor. My daughter found them irritating. Go figure.

There are as many types of humor as there are people. Some jokes are based on putting ourselves down and may draw a sympathetic chuckle from the audience, who can recall once making the same mistake themselves. But many jokes are based on putting others down as groups, perpetuating stereotypes and mining them for humor. Stereotypes are anything but funny. Although as humans we classify each person or thing we encounter based on similarities to previous experiences, stereotyping leads us right into the trap of underestimating or prejudging people; and that basic error will be quickly compounded into distrust and miscommunication.

In these days of concern about being politically correct, many people understand that a joke based on racial stereotypes is not acceptable in a business setting. They will not tell the joke at work, even if they might tell that same joke to a family member or a neighbor. That split between work and home takes its toll, however. There is the stress of being insincere in one context or the other, the fear of making a slip, and the nagging feeling at the edge of your conscience that you are not being fair.

There are other challenges with humor. You may feel personally at ease telling a Polish joke because you are of Polish ancestry. That doesn't mean your listener will find it funny or admire you for laughing at your own heritage. The sad truth is that every racial or ethnic joke is based on an assumption, that the group being joked about is inferior and has undesirable traits. Some groups get labeled as drunkards or being cheap, but nearly all groups get tagged with being slow, lazy, and not very smart. That's why jokes that were told about the British troops during the Revolutionary War were retold in the North about southerners during the Civil War, and again by whites about native Americans during the Indian wars. That's why Irish jokes about "Pat and Mike" get retold in Minnesota as "Ole and Lena," and in Milwaukee as "Hans and Hilda." Today, to avoid a charge of ethnic insensitivity, many of these have been recycled as "blonde" jokes, but they are all based on the assumption that the subject is unintelligent or lazy or both.

Sometimes we justify a stereotype by citing how many exceptions to it we personally know. This is the "some of my best friends are" response. A good example of that is Dolly Parton's response when asked if it bothered her to hear jokes about dumb blondes. She replied with her usual candor, "Of course not. I know I'm not a blonde." While many people might laugh at group stereotype humor, thinking to themselves, "I'm not like that," many others will cringe inside and wonder how the teller could be so insensitive or unaware.

What about jokes about other professions? The spate of lawyer and stockbroker jokes a few years back are good examples. What's the harm? Well, they are probably no more damaging than the generations of jokes about salespeople. How funny are those to you? Do you enjoy having someone you meet at a social gathering immediately start backing away from you when he or she finds out you are in sales? Or start to tell you just exactly what he or she thinks of salespeople in general? Whenever we perpetuate stereotypes, we impede rather than enhance developing genuine understanding and communication.

How can we respond to humor we find offensive without creating a rift in the group or getting labeled as thin-skinned or having no sense of humor? One good response is simply to say "ouch" and let it go at that. The joke teller with any awareness of his or her audience will pick up on your discomfort. For repeat offenders, though, all you can do is talk to them one-on-one and ask them to refrain from making racist or other offensive comments. Some companies have ombudsmen or other anonymous ways to report repeat offenders; and, remember, the law considers creating a hostile environment in the workplace to be harassment.

Life is funny. Human beings are funny—and never so much as when we are taking ourselves too seriously. Humor is best as a discovery, a surprise, a moment of shared laughter at a sudden realization or a situation or a misstatement. You both suddenly look up and start to laugh. You can't help yourselves. Those moments are precious. They rarely happen when forced.

Golf Outings and Other Social Situations

Sales managers encourage their salespeople to entertain customers in the belief that it builds relationships and loyalties that result in good account control. Many activities, such as taking a customer golfing or getting tickets to the big game, have become traditional sales tools. Lunches and dinners at expensive restaurants, combined with large drink tabs, have been another popular bonding activity. Many customers enjoy these outings and look forward to them. Others, however, prefer to spend their evenings at home with their families, rather than out with their sales representative, no matter how much they might enjoy his or her company. It is important to know your customer's preference, as well as to make sure you are not shortchanging your own family in order to satisfy your sales manager.

One young sales engineer I know recently had an open discussion with each of her key customers. She told them she was committed to being efficient and prepared when she visited them so that their own time was not wasted and they could get home by 5:30 p.m. She was not going to be the reason they had to work late. Her customers were delighted with her approach and reciprocated with a commitment that they, too, would be prepared and efficient in dealing with her so she didn't have to work late evenings or weekends to make up for their springing a surprise on her at the last minute.

If you and your customer agree that a golf outing or fishing trip or a night at the game would be fun for both of you, remember that it is social. It does not create obligation for the customer. It does not require payback. It should be offered by you as a gift, no strings attached. If business is conducted, it should be brief and to the point. The primary purpose should be the time spent together and the strengthening of the relationship. If you offer these outings hoping to create obligation or payback, you have just gone from a social outing to a bribe.

So many companies are concerned these days about creating even the appearance of impropriety that gifts to their employees from suppliers are discouraged and, in some cases, strictly regulated. For example, many purchasing professionals are no longer allowed to receive what marketing people refer to as "trash and trinkets." Coffee mugs and pens with your company logo, desk clocks, leather portfolios, or other items are commonly given out by salespeople to their customers. Today, many companies require that all gifts, regardless of cash value, have to be reported. Others require that gifts in excess of $25.00 must be returned; or, if returning the gift would result in a severe loss of face to the giver, it must be donated to charity in the company's name. Even the cost of lunch or dinner must be reported at some companies, with their employees obligated to pay their own way.

It is important that you know and respect the rules so that your well-meaning gesture doesn't create a problem for your customer. Many purchasing departments have pamphlets printed up that list the rules concerning gifts. If you are not able to give gifts but want to show appreciation to your customers, there are other options you can choose. Bring a tray of home-baked cookies into the department for everyone to share, or set up a barbecue out in the parking lot at noon for the department employees. Holding an open house at your own facility and inviting your customers to come and bring their families is another. And don't forget: a handwritten note or a card is always appreciated as a thank you, sometimes far more than just another desk clock.

Are Strip Clubs Sales Tools?

There are still salesmen who believe that they must take their customers to a sex club or strip joint because their customers expect it. If your customer expects you to host his trip to such a place, the chances are good that he is also using you as his excuse for going, and you are the bad guy as far as his family is concerned. Even men who frequent such places on their own time don't brag about it to their wives or their ministers or their children and for good reason: No matter how titillating they may find the experience, they recognize that it is viewed as morally wrong, or at least questionable, by many people. If you wouldn't feel comfortable telling your children all about it, why in the world do it?

Some companies have recently stated that sexually oriented entertainment is not acceptable as a business entertainment choice. In some cases, they have refused to reimburse expense reports submitted by salesmen for such activities. But whether your company has a rule about it or not, the acid test is still whether you feel pride or shame when escorting customers in these situations. If deep down inside you're hoping no one sees you, you shouldn't be there in the first place.

When I was a global sales manager, I often hosted groups of foreign visitors, some of whom expected us to provide entertainment, including "girls." I was told by my sales managers that it is important to provide whatever the customer expects and that different cultures have different moral standards. While it is certainly true that every culture has its own moral standards, there is a universal truth that outweighs any ethnocentric view. If I am morally compromised by the activity, I am obligated not to participate. My customers may go off and do whatever they choose to on their own time and on their own travel budgets. I am no more obligated to host their sexual adventures than I would be to buy them cocaine. I have never had a customer decide not to do business with me because I wouldn't support his recreational activities. In fact, I am convinced I have earned respect for my commitment to my principles. Of course, I have not lectured, judged, or condemned the customers for their choices. It is not my place to make their moral decisions for them. I am responsible, however, for my own decisions and for making sure they are consistent with my soul's needs.

In general, alcohol consumption has decreased among salespeople and selling situations for many reasons: awareness of the danger of drinking and driving, fear of liability suits, increased concerns about health, increased awareness of addiction, and more. The days of the three-martini lunch are over, and even when an event involves social drinking, a designated driver is appointed by the wise salesperson. When a large event is being held, it is becoming customary to provide a bus or a shuttle for the customers, so that they don't have to choose between drinking and driving. If you drink during a business event, it is essential to know your own limits and to remember that it is business first and foremost. You must be clearheaded and ready for questions or for discussions that arise. It's similar to hosting a party in that the comfort of your guests comes first, and the "FHB or family hold back" rule dictates that you put your own enjoyment second to taking care of the customer.

Drugs are illegal. Period. You may never have to deal with this question; but if you do, remember that whatever your personal views on the subject, the government has spoken. If you choose to indulge with your customers or to provide them with drugs, you are sending a much larger message than you think. "I'm an easygoing fun kind of person who doesn't get too uptight about stuff" might be what you want to say. But you are also saying loudly and clearly, "I break laws. I don't think the rules should apply to me. I have no respect for the law. I don't let ethics get in the way of a good time."

Like most people, you may think of yourself as someone who hates giving speeches, but your actions and your choices are speaking for you all the time. Without even realizing it, most of us are loud, effective, and convincing public speakers—without saying a word.

REFLECTIONS ON CHAPTER 14
Temptations and Compromising Situations

Don't compromise yourself. You are all you've got.
—Janis Joplin

It is hard to resist peer pressure and to live in a way that is consistent with what we most value. But when we do step outside our own moral and spiritual beliefs, we pay the price physically and emotionally. Ask yourself the following questions:

1. How would your coworkers describe your ethics? Your customers? Your spouse or partner? Your children?
2. What makes you laugh? Are there messages there for you about your values? Your prejudices?
3. Are you walking your talk? Do your actions ring true with what you say you believe in?
4. Have you compartmentalized your life into separate areas with separate rules? For example, in business do you follow a "When in Rome, do as the Romans do" code, while with your children you practice "Do as I say, not as I do"?
5. When is the last time you admitted to making a mistake? How did it feel? What could you have learned from it by analyzing it openly and seeking feedback?

Note to Self: I choose to stand up for my values.

CHAPTER 15

The Importance Of Spiritual Role Models

I ONCE TAUGHT A workshop on giving an effective presentation. My audience consisted of middle and high school students who voluntarily participate in a program called M.E.S.A. (mathematics, engineering, and scientific achievement), which includes after-school and Saturday leadership classes. The group is bright, highly motivated, and focused on achieving academic success. I asked them to think of a speaker they admired, either alive or dead. They stared back at me with blank faces. I asked them to name an inspiring leader. Again, no response. I began tossing out names to break the ice.

"How about Dr. Martin Luther King, Jr.? Abraham Lincoln? John F. Kennedy?" While they agreed with those suggestions, they were still at a loss to add names.

"How about your minister? Your basketball coach? Your grandmother? Anyone in your life who can inspire you when they speak to you?" I asked.

Bringing it closer to home helped a bit, and several of the students were able to talk about a time when someone had inspired them with a few well-timed words. Although we humans learn best by doing and following another's example, there was a void where there should have been inspiring leaders, role models, and spiritual coaches.

For the next several weeks, I scanned the news reports in print and on television, looking for material I could bring into the class. News reports did a good job of showing us what *not* to do, covering political and sexual scandal and violent crime in lurid detail. Anyone recently exposed for his or her sins found a microphone jammed in his face in short order. Except for a thirty-second "happy spot" of news at the end of each broadcast, there was little to give hope and inspiration.

The most upbeat stories I found seemed to single out athletes for attention. Michael Jordan, Venus and Serena Williams, Wayne Gretzky, and many others have our respect for breaking records in their sports and setting new standards of performance, but isn't there more to admire in our society than athletic prowess?

Even people who were deeply committed to living their principles and practicing compassion, often at great personal sacrifice, appear newsworthy only when they die. Mother Teresa's death was nearly overshadowed by Princess Diana's. Princess Diana herself worked tirelessly on behalf of charities and AIDS research, and yet the news coverage of her life spent little time on her work, spotlighting instead the personal tragedies of her life. We have lost something precious if all we report is what one tabloid describes as what "Enquiring" minds want to know.

Where are our living role models? I am not advocating hero worship. Human beings are wonderfully complex creatures, with all the failings and contradictions that make us unique. I am not suggesting we return to the unwritten rules that kept the press from reporting on FDR's mistress in the White House or photographing Jacqueline Kennedy with a cigarette. But, like many baby boomers, I mourn the loss of ideals. In his song "Mrs. Robinson," Paul Simon grieves, "Where have you gone, Joe DiMaggio? A nation turns its lonely eyes to you." We are a nation expecting our heroes will be caught, literally and figuratively, with their pants down. How terribly sad if all we can find to admire in our leaders is a carefully crafted illusion manufactured by press agents.

Keeping our words and actions consistent with our values is difficult. When we are first hushed as children for saying out loud what the adults are only thinking, we begin a lifelong education in social compromise. The little white lies we justify to spare someone's feelings too often grow up into big, self-serving whoppers created to avoid the consequences of our choices. We start out learning the Ten Commandments or the Golden Rule and, over the years, replace them with situational ethics or a "safety in numbers" rationale that "everyone's doing it." Speeding down a highway at eighty miles per hour, ignoring the posted limit of sixty-five, we tell ourselves we're just keeping up with traffic. If we're the unlucky one singled out and pulled over by the state police, we are angered at the unfairness of it all.

This is why my parents were fond of saying, "Do as I say, not as I do," and why I cringed when the same words came out of my own mouth years later and my daughter reacted with a puzzled frown. When Tina Turner sings, "We don't need another hero," she expresses the pain we share in having heroes disappoint us. Yet we do need heroes and heroines. We need to see values modeled, not just preached. A part of us longs to sit at the feet of someone we admire, a master, and learn the right way to live. But where do we turn for guidance?

Tina Turner is herself a heroine and role model, as someone who overcame difficult circumstances and succeeded. She publicly acknowledges her daily practice of Buddhist meditation and spiritual contemplation as important elements in keeping her personal and professional lives in harmony. Others turn to religion as a guide. Despite our American slogan of "In God we trust," surveys show we are not a nation of churchgoers, and membership in many churches is declining with each generation. Yet every day of our lives, we need coaching and guidance and support if we are to live in harmony with our beliefs. Where are we to find it?

Cartoon images often show an angel on one shoulder and a devil on the other, each trying to convince the character to do it their way. If only it were so clear! But each of us has a conscience, and it is sometimes easier to personify that voice by attaching it to a role model. Since values are invisible except through behavior, one way to begin building our own support system is to list people we admire. Who do you look to as a spiritual leader or role model? Who inspires you?

Pendants and pins bearing four initials, WWJD, have been popular with Christians. They stand for the phrase "What would Jesus do?" and are worn as reminders to live in accordance with their faith each day. For Christians, Jesus is God, but because he came to earth in human form, he is also a human role model. In addition to studying his teachings, Christians can look to the life of Jesus in the Holy Bible to provide an example of how to live. His behavior included acts of healing and charity, acts of rebelling against self-serving commerce and hypocrisy, and acts of compassion and sacrifice.

But you don't have to be a Christian to use the example of "WWJD" as a guide. You can create or identify your own role models from people you admire and, when you are facing a moral challenge, ask yourself what they would do. My own list of people I admire as moral leaders includes Buddha, Gandhi, Dr. Martin Luther King, Jr., Cesar Chavez, Oprah Winfrey, Margaret Mead, Sojourner Truth, Stephen Covey, Eleanor Roosevelt, and more. None of them was perfect, but each sincerely tried to put their beliefs into practice and to live in a consistently spiritual and loving way.

How about you? Some of the names that have come up in my discussions with others may stimulate your own thought processes: The Reverend Jesse Jackson, Mother Teresa, Maimonides, Ruth from the Holy Bible, Saint Elisabeth Seton, Rabbi Harold Kushner, the Prophet Mohammed, Malcolm X, Joseph Smith, Rumi, the Dalai Lama, Thich Nhat Hanh, Abraham Lincoln.

Your list may include new age teachers like Deepak Chopra, scientists like Carl Sagan, or creators of science fiction like George Lucas. It can include writers or favorite characters from fiction or the movies, like Yoda, the Jedi master from *Star Wars,* or Atticus Finch in *To Kill a Mockingbird*. Or maybe it's made up of teachers you remember or your next-door neighbor, who has the sunniest of attitudes on the grayest of days. The list can include anyone whose behavior gives clear and convincing testimony to his or her values—values you share.

Several years ago, newspapers reported that Secretary of State Hillary Clinton had imaginary conversations with the ghost of Eleanor Roosevelt. Clinton explained that she often sorts out complex issues by imagining a dialogue with someone whose opinion she admires and respects. I find this technique valuable as well. Whether you carry on imaginary debates with a hero or use the pages of a journal to work out the many sides of a complex issue, the more we engage our conscience, the more it becomes a habit. Like exercising a tired muscle makes it stronger, engaging in debate with what Abraham Lincoln referred to as the "better angels" of our nature makes them more accessible to us as we face the difficult decisions of each business day. Taking a tip from the stars and celebrities who have a personal trainer to keep them motivated and fit, I sometimes picture one of my role models sitting on my "angel" shoulder prepared to duke it out with my own devils of rationalization, selfishness, laziness, and greed.

When I am stumped as to what my role model would do or what he or she would offer as guidance in a situation, I fall back on the opposite approach. I picture Mike Wallace and the film crew from *Sixty Minutes* sitting on my "devil" shoulder getting ready to broadcast my behavior.

Imagining how my good intentions would appear if reported through unforgiving cynical eyes can be a shock. My worst failings in bold print headlines! If that's not enough motivation for doing the right thing, I take a breath and pray. Or at least, take a break. Sometimes we're too close to the situation to see our way clear to the best solution. Taking some time to back off always helps. I have learned, through my many mistakes, that it may take more time to do the right thing than my impatient self would like; but it always takes less time to do it right than to fix it after I do it wrong.

REFLECTIONS ON CHAPTER 15
The Importance of Spiritual Role Models

There are only two ways of spreading light—to be the candle or the mirror that reflects it.
—Edith Wharton

Whom do you admire? Who exhibits qualities you wish you had as well? Ask yourself the following questions to help identify people, living or dead, whom you want in your pantheon of role models.

1. List as many people as you can whom you admire. Don't worry about whether you admire them for their accomplishments, their words, or their effect on history—just list them.

2. Look over your list and see what words you come up with to describe these people. For example, Rosa Parks might be on your list because she was courageous, or Albert Einstein might be on your list because he embodies intellectual curiosity and genius. List the qualities in a column.

3. The qualities you list are indications of your values. Check the ones that you believe apply to you as well. Can you think of a particular example from your own life where your behavior showed that same quality? Begin to recognize in yourself examples of these admirable qualities, and then reinforce your own behavior. Don't hesitate to give yourself a mental pat on the back.

4. If there are qualities you believe you lack, or others of which you are not proud, don't waste time beating yourself up for them. Instead, recognize that we are here to learn and to grow, and each of us is a work in process. You will have opportunities to make different decisions in the future. Be prepared to reinforce and celebrate those when they occur.

5. Remember that no one is perfect. Even our heroes will disappoint us from time to time. Tiger Woods, John Edwards, or some other public figure may let you down. Forgive them as you forgive yourself your own failings, and then remind yourself to do better and to strive for consistency.

Note to Self: Progress, not perfection, is my motto.

AFTERWORD

A Few Final Thoughts

Every time you suppress some part of yourself or allow others to play you small, you are in essence ignoring the owner's manual your creator gave you and destroying your design.
—Oprah Winfrey

EVERY DAY IS A new opportunity to live a life we are proud of and to show by our choices what we value most. Old habits die hard. As important as taking care of our bodies by choosing nourishing food and exercising regularly is keeping our spiritual health on our agenda. If we aspire to Bob's balance, we need to remind ourselves to differentiate the important from the urgent. We need to practice the qualities of selling with soul shared in chapter one and throughout this book:

- Enjoying a balanced life where work and family behavior are congruent
- Recognizing the importance of empathy
- Respecting yourself and your customer
- Practicing persistence and patience
- Listening to yourself and others with sensitivity
- Avoiding rationalization
- Embracing change
- Being a lifelong learner
- Achieving philosophical alignment

We need to develop new habits and new rituals. Finding the ones that work for you is an essential part of living and selling with soul. Some of the rituals for daily renewal that work for me—when I work them—and that have helped others I know to be their best are offered here to get you started thinking of your own:

- Praying and meditating daily.
- Reading inspirational texts.
- Writing a gratitude list at the end of the day of five things you're thankful for.
- Writing a goal for each day or week and posting it on your mirror.
- Taking five minutes each morning to think about what you most want to accomplish that day.
- Writing in your day planner what is most important to you so you can do what matters most.
- Making sure your goals include personal and family goals, not just business goals.
- Finding some regular time to visit with, or to talk with, your spiritual mentor or coach.
- Finding a support network of people who share your principles and values.
- Practicing forgiveness of people who have hurt you or disappointed you.
- Making amends to people you have hurt or disappointed.
- Regularly asking for guidance when you face challenges and obstacles, whether you go inside yourself or to your God or to a Higher Power you trust.
- Regularly giving thanks for all the blessings in your life.

As you take each step in your journey, I wish you all love and success and spiritual growth. May each day be a blessing.

A Gift for my Readers

You can share your reaction to this book and ask questions by joining a free one-hour teleconference discussion with the author. For more information, please check the website www.sparkercoaching.com for times and sign-up information.

BIBLIOGRAPHY

Those books in the following list that were not referenced in the text provide good reading material to support your ongoing efforts to sell with soul.

Blanchard, Kenneth H., and Spencer Johnson. (1981) *The One Minute Manager*. New York: William Morrow & Company.
Bosworth, Michael T. (2004) *Solution Selling: Creating Customers in Difficult Selling Markets*. New York: McGraw-Hill.
Bosworth, Michael T., John R. Holland, and Frank Visgatis. (1984) *CustomerCentric Selling*. New York: McGraw-Hill.
Canfield, Jack, and Mark Victor Hanson. (1993) *Chicken Soup for the Soul: 101 Stories to Open the Heart and Rekindle the Spirit*. Deerfield Beach, FL: Health Communications.
Covey, Stephen R. (1990) *The 7 Habits of Highly Effective People*. New York: Fireside Press.
Drucker, Peter F. (1999) *Management Challenges for the 21st Century*. New York: HarperCollins.
Gray, John. (1992) *Men Are from Mars, Women Are from Venus*. New York: HarperCollins.
Heiman, Stephen E., Tad Tuleja, Robert B. Miller, and J. W. Marriott. (1998) *The New Strategic Selling: The Unique Sales System Proven Successful by the World's Best Companies*. New York: Warner Books.
Holland, John R., and Tim Young. (2010) *Rethinking the Sales Cycle. How Superior Sellers Embrace the Buying Cycle to Achieve a Sustainable and Competitive Advantage*. New York: McGraw Hill.

Hopkins, Tom. (1980) *How to Master the Art of Selling*. New York: Warner Books.

Johnson, Spencer. (1984) *The One Minute $ales Person*. New York: William Morrow & Company.

Konrath, Jill. (2006) *Selling to Big Companies*. New York: Dearborn Trade Publishing.

Kotler, Philip, and Kevin Lane Keller. (2002) *Marketing Management*. Upper Saddle River, NJ: Prentice Hall.

Molloy, John T. (1988) *Dress for Success*. New York: Warner Books.

Moore, Geoffrey. (1995) *Inside the Tornado: Strategies for Developing, Leveraging, and Surviving Hypergrowth Markets*. New York: HarperCollins.

Morgen, Sharon Drew. (1999) *Selling with Integrity: Reinventing Sales through Collaboration, Respect, and Serving*. San Francisco: Berrett-Koehler.

Peters, Thomas J., and Robert H. Waterman. (1982) *In Search of Excellence*. New York: HarperCollins.

Rackham, Neil. (1988) *SPIN Selling*. New York: McGraw-Hill.

Rosen, Keith. (2008) *Coaching Salespeople Into Sales Champions: A Tactical Playbook for Managers and Executives*. Hoboken, NJ: John Wiley & Sons.

Scott, Susan. (2002) *Fierce Conversations: Achieving Success at Work and in Life One Conversation at a Time*. San Francisco: The Berkley Publishing Company.

Tannen, Deborah. (1991) *You Just Don't Understand: Women and Men in Conversation*. New York: HarperCollins.

Tracy, Brian. (2007) *The Art of Closing Sales: The Key to Making More Money Faster in the World of Professional Selling*. New York: Thomas Nelson, Inc.

Wilson, Orvel Ray, William K. Gallagher, and Jay Conrad Levinson. (1992) *Guerrilla Selling: Unconventional Weapons and Tactics for Increasing Your Sales*. New York: Houghton Mifflin.

Ziglar, Zig. (2000) *See You at the Top*. Gretna, LA: Pelican.

Open Book Editions
A Berrett-Koehler Partner

OPEN BOOK EDITIONS is a joint venture between Berrett-Koehler Publishers and Author Solutions, the market leader in self-publishing. There are many more aspiring authors who share Berrett-Koehler's mission than we can sustainably publish. To serve these authors, Open Book Editions offers a comprehensive self-publishing opportunity.

A Shared Mission

Open Book Editions welcomes authors who share the Berrett-Koehler mission—Creating a World That Works for All. We believe that to truly create a better world, action is needed at all levels—individual, organizational, and societal. At the individual level, our publications help people align their lives with their values and with their aspirations for a better world. At the organizational level, we promote progressive leadership and management practices, socially responsible approaches to business, and humane and effective organizations. At the societal level, we publish content that advances social and economic justice, shared prosperity, sustainability, and new solutions to national and global issues.

Open Book Editions represents a new way to further the BK mission and expand our community. . We look forward to helping more authors challenge conventional thinking, introduce new ideas, and foster positive change.

For more information, see the Open Book Editions website:

http://www.iuniverse.com/Packages/OpenBookEditions.aspx

Join the BK Community! See exclusive author videos, join discussion groups, find out about upcoming events, read author blogs, and much more!

http://bkcommunity.com/

www.ingramcontent.com/pod-product-compliance
Lightning Source LLC
Chambersburg PA
CBHW031056180526
45163CB00002BA/861